PORTRAIT
of a
MESTIZA

PORTRAIT *of a* MESTIZA

A MEMOIR IN ESSAYS

Marianna Marlowe

SHE WRITES PRESS

Published in 2026 by
She Writes Press, an imprint of The Stable Book Group

SWP

32 Court Street, Suite 2109
Brooklyn, NY 11201
https://shewritespress.com
Library of Congress Control Number: 2026900403
ISBN: 979-8-89636-100-8
eISBN: 979-8-89636-101-5

Printed in the United States

Names and identifying characteristics have been changed to protect the privacy of certain individuals.

To Gloria Anzaldúa, *mestiza extraordinaria*:
my role model, my hero.

Author's Note

The essays in this collection were written over the past seven years. Because the book is organized thematically rather than chronologically, the narrative perspective—the "now" of each piece—shifts throughout. Readers may notice that certain individuals, most notably my parents, are described using the present tense in early essays and the past tense in later ones. This reflects the passage of time, as I lost both my parents during the period in which these essays were written.

CONTENTS

PART THREE: INNOCENCE LOST

I am an act of kneading, of uniting and joining that not only has produced both a creature of darkness and a creature of light, but also a creature that questions the definitions of light and dark and gives them new meanings.

The answer to the problem between the white race and the colored, between males and females, lies in healing the split that originates in the very foundation of our lives, our culture, our languages, our thoughts. A massive uprooting of dualistic thinking in the individual and collective consciousness is the beginning of a long struggle, but one that could in our best hopes, bring us to the end of rape, of violence, of war.

Because the future depends on the breaking down of paradigms, it depends on the straddling of two or more cultures. By creating a new mythos—that is, a change in the way we perceive reality, the way we see ourselves, and the ways we behave—la mestiza creates a new consciousness.

—Gloria Anzaldúa

PROLOGUE:

Malinche's Legacy

I LOOKED WITH SATISFACTION IN the mirror. It was 1978, the second year in my family's four-year residence in Ecuador, a sojourn undertaken for my father to work for the international division of his engineering company. It was Halloween, and the students of my middle school in Quito were excited to go to classes in costumes. My own costume had been entirely my idea and I was proud of it. My eleven-year-old reflection gazed complacently back at me that day before the school bus stopped at our gate.

What I saw in the mirror was a young face divided in half. My mother, who must have been humoring me in what she thought was a quaint experiment, had drawn, with black eyebrow pencil, a thin dark line from the middle parting high on my forehead all the way down, as straight and undeviating as possible, to the bottom of my chin. My hair had been similarly divided and a long braid hung heavily over my left shoulder. This same side was bare, devoid of makeup and unadorned by jewelry. On the other side, my right side, my hair had been brushed and straightened so that it hung in a smooth curtain. On this side my face had been powdered white, the right half of my mouth lipsticked a sophisticated red, my right ear decorated with a gold hoop earring. There I stood—half Indigenous, half Spanish: *una mestiza*.

For my mother, *mestiza* was a dirty word.

MALINCHE, MALINALI, MALINTZÍN, Marina. She has been labeled La Malinche, the Mexican Eve, and Mother of the Mestizos. History categorizes her as an Aztec princess by birth and a slave by circumstance, as a talented interpreter on the one hand and a wife and concubine on the other. Was she victim or traitor, warrior or whore?

Like North America's Pocahontas, Malinche acted as a bridge—culturally, sexually, and linguistically—between two alien cultures: the Old World and the New, the conquering and the conquered. But unlike Pocahontas, Malinche has been vilified as temptress and traitor. There isn't a Disney cartoon depicting a beautiful-but-modest, strong-but-helpful Native woman who befriends the well-meaning European hero, himself manly and blond, to facilitate the safe settlement of the newcomers in the lush and fertile territory. Such depictions gloss over any betrayal of community, tribe, or culture on the part of Pocahontas, erasing uncomfortable histories of conquest and genocide, exploitation and treaty-breaking.

The internet is rife with images of La Malinche in paintings, murals, videos, and films. A bumpy-cover romance heroine with red lips, shiny hair, and Anglo features. An ethnic pulp-fiction sex symbol: voluptuous, clad in a scanty Native costume, legs and cleavage front and center. A more realistic depiction: brown skin, black hair, wide nose, thick lips, but still feminine, still sexualized. More recently: a warrior woman, a militarized mother, a historically recuperated leader of a colonized people.

To this day my mother and my Peruvian relatives, like most of their class, deny any Indigenous ancestry, embracing instead their Spanish heritage. If asked, my mother, my grandmother, my aunts and uncles and cousins, are quick to claim European ancestry: *Mi bisabuela era Española* or *Mi bisabuelo vino de España*. We traffic, like the biblical Peter, in denial. We deny our legacy, our heritage, our mothers. A son of one of my cousins came out dark and black-eyed; another cousin's son, born the same year, came out blond and green-eyed. Until he reached adulthood, the dark boy's nickname was *el guardaespaldas*; it was a joke in my family that the brown boy looked like the bodyguard of the fair one. When will the cock crow the third and final time? If it does, will it wake us at last from this denial that rejects our shared humanity? Will it jolt us from our entitlement so that we cease to live a cruel brand of racism? Will we, like the apostle, finally acknowledge our self-serving lies?

In the colonialist rhetoric of European purity that dominates South American countries today, white blood has been tainted by Native blood. The white identity, innately superior, has been corrupted by the brown. *Los indios* are dirty and ignorant. They don't deserve big houses and imported cars, pools and vacations, or education and a viable income. They are good only for the servitude that they, since the days of the *conquistadores*, were born into. This prejudice is sustainable in part because class, despite the colonialist history of interracial coupling, remains visible in Peru. The poor tend to be darker and shorter, the rich taller and paler. The body dictates destiny.

My hair is unique, as a color expert once informed me, in tone, depth, and blackness, to only a few groups of people on the planet, one of them the Indigenous Peruvians. The color of my hair binds me directly to my mestiza heritage, to a thread of my DNA that leads back over the centuries to the first mestizos and thus, ultimately, to women like La Malinche herself. As mistress of, as well as interpreter for, the Spanish conquistador Hernán Cortés, Malinche bore his mestizo son, Martín. Is this thread a chain or a lifeline? My mother would see it as a chain, something imprisoning, something enslaving, because of what it shackles us to; she would see me, her daughter, darker-skinned and black-haired like her, forever chained to this identity, despised and repudiated: *una mestiza*.

My aunt shakes her head at me conspiratorially. I've just recounted the story of my conversation with the hair colorist. Visiting my family in Northern California, she sits with me by the lavender and bougainvillea on my flagstone patio one cool spring morning, the view of the green valley and glimpses of the San Francisco Bay stretching before us. Wearing blue silk, diamonds flashing in the sunlight, and a mink stole gleaming sleekly around her shoulders, my aunt speaks dismissively. "*¿Qué estuvo pensando esa señora sonsa?*" What was that silly woman thinking? "*Tu pelo es negro porque eres italiana como tu abuelo, ¡no porque eres como las indias!*" She tells me that my hair is black because I'm Italian like my grandfather. She refuses any link to the Indigenous, to the women exploited and raped by the Spanish men who came to conquer the New World, to *las indias* who were instruments in the colonization of entire cultures, Mayan and Aztec and Incan, mostly as the unwilling progenitors of a new race: the mestizos.

Along with fairy tales of sleeping princesses and rescuing princes, little girls in red capes and wolves hidden in forest shadows, or mermaid sacrifices and enchanted beasts, I was raised with stories of aristocratic ancestry, familial position, and inherited status. From my mother's and my grandmother's lips, I heard the legend of my great-grandfather's hacienda and my great-grandmother's

Hispanicness. A grandfather's Italianness. This same grandfather's emigration from Piombino to Lima. His mica mines that—for a while, at least—reinforced my family's class superiority by providing vast new wealth. My mother and aunt's upbringing in the countryside, which included a governess who sat by her young charges for formal meals separate from the adults, a tall black horse called Moro my mother rode as he galloped through orchards of mangoes, and the beloved Great Dane who teased her and her sister on walks by abruptly and unexpectedly blocking their path with his massive girth.

In addition to fairy-tale illustrations of ogres and knights, I grew up entertained by the black-and-white photographs taken in the 1940s and '50s of my mother's family in Peru. In one series, my mother and aunt, perhaps five and eight years old, sit closely, heads touching gently, huge silk bows drooping over their black hair. This image dramatizes their whiteness and their affluence. There is a second photograph, one I consider the polar opposite of the first, in which my mother and her sister are outfitted in Native Andean dress. Wearing felt hats, embroidered capes, and full skirts topped with thick woolen jackets, they hold carved gourds and bamboo panpipes in their small hands. They stand in front of an artificial set depicting in miniature the jutting mountains and terraced hills of Machu Picchu. It's clear to me that my grandmother, despite her flat cheekbones, wide nose, and almond eyes, was secure enough then to play with identity through costume and masquerade, to dress her girls in the Indigenous clothing of the Andes—a performance that, in its very enactment, rendered the possibility of Native ancestry preposterous while simultaneously reifying as fact her daughters' pure white blood.

During the years we spent in Ecuador, my siblings and my mother and I gathered most evenings to watch telenovelas.

"Hurry! It's about to start!" we called to each other, loath to miss even one minute of the exciting plot. We three children then clambered onto my parents' bed while my father read his newspaper alone in the living room, and snuggled together with my mother under the covers to watch *Colorina* or *Los Ricos También Lloran* or *Andrea Celeste*.

Obsessed with the limpid-eyed and glossy-haired beauty of the telenovelas' protagonists, I tracked the heroines' every move, took note of their every outfit, admired their jewelry and makeup and hairstyles. Even when playing mestizas, the actresses cast for these parts were invariably light-skinned and Anglo-featured. As a tween and teen navigating puberty, I fantasized about inhabiting the bodies of these young women, trying fruitlessly to mimic their mannerisms, to move and gesture in the ways they did, the ways I found admirably sophisticated. Nightly I stared at Colorina's lustrous lips and perfectly waved red hair. I wished I had the pert nose and stick-straight ponytail of the actress who played the young orphan girl Andrea Celeste. I wanted for myself both the brunette beauty of the mother in *Los Ricos También Lloran* and the blonde perfection of her daughter.

But along with beauty tips, I, ever the enthusiastic student, also absorbed a culture in which white was superior to brown, European was better than Native, the upper class was more desirable and, ultimately, worthy than the lower class. The rich might also cry, I learned, but they did so in luxury and style.

I see now that when I dressed up for Halloween all those years ago by dividing my body in two, by demarcating the strict boundaries between the conflicting halves constituting the identity of the mestiza, I, like my grandmother, was playing with cultural signification, with brownness and whiteness, with power and objectification. It was not that I felt safe from, or untouched by, or above the disempowerment of the colonized, but that I didn't know *not* to feel that way. Still an innocent, I unconsciously inhabited the cocoon of privilege granted me by my Anglo father, my US citizenship, my relatively fair skin, my youth. Yet, looking back, I see that on that Halloween I, too, performed race; I rehearsed, because I could afford to, a masquerade of mestizaje.

Later, in my twenties, when I became conscious of La Malinche as a historical figure and cultural icon, I still retained a vaguely negative impression of her. A Proustian experience in sound and syllable rather than tongue and taste, her name evokes, to my ear, negativity, even perversity. "Mal" in Spanish means bad, sick, or wrong. Even though I've discovered that "Malinche" is the Spanish pronunciation of the Aztec "Malintzín," the name given to her at birth, and that the Catholic conquerors renamed her Marina—a derivation of María, the Mother of God in Christian lore—the sound of her name still conjures for me the damning labels of traitor, temptress, sellout, whore.

By now I've learned a new perspective, a politicized one, a recuperative one, one that counteracts any negative connotation to the sound of La Malinche's name still lingering in my unconscious. Chicana scholar Gloria Anzaldúa theorized a mestizaje that empowers because it is stronger in its hybridity, embodying the potential in admixture versus the weakness in inbreeding. Instead of defining ourselves against the Other, we, *las mestizas*—the dark and the light, the brown and the white—hold within our raced and gendered identity the rejection of divisive binaries, of superior/inferior, us/them, colonizer/colonized, European/Indigenous, Spanish/Native, male/female. *La mestiza* promises an alternative consciousness, a third space, a new way of thinking—beyond binaries—that lies latent in our very DNA.

What does this mean for me?

I have become another kind of mestiza. On the one hand, I see La Malinche's legacy in my own life. Her role as interpreter echoes and reverberates in all mestizas, including myself, who with our bodies and our experiences serve as bridges, as translators, between brown and white, between identities and communities and cultures. I value this heritage; I accept this responsibility. Yet the liberating potential in a mestiza consciousness, first embraced in my twenties, cannot erase the profound acculturation of my earlier years. I exist in a limbo that painfully negotiates between my identification with the culture of my mother, an identification difficult to separate from my love for her, and my allegiance to a philosophy of inclusion and equality rather than hierarchies and divisions. I try, through my actions and my words, in conversations and with my writing, to embody this alternative identity, to model this new ideal—the politicized mestiza. I have to acknowledge, however, that my attempts are flawed. Always, haunting my memories, shadowing my thoughts, and mediating my decisions is my mother—my first and longest love, I cannot abandon her. For me, *la mestiza* is a hybrid identity that forever contradicts itself, one that I inhabit, Janus-faced, every day, month after month, year after year. I do not know if I will ever be free. Perhaps this is the dark side of privilege for me—my pound of flesh, the price I must pay.

I DON'T RECALL—AT LEAST NOT with the precision I remember admiring the mirror's reflection of my made-up face—the reaction at my middle school that Halloween morning. Certainly not the reactions of the other children. It may be that they didn't understand the nuances of my costume. I wonder today how I came to have that idea: representing with makeup, jewelry, and hairstyle a biracial, bicultural identity.

Did I pick it up during a class when we studied the history of the Americas? Because I know we studied not only Ecuador but also all the other countries, from Mexico to Argentina—including Peru, my mother's homeland. It must have been in school then, in history or social studies. Where else could it have been, if my mother never pronounced—as if it were a curse—the word *mestiza*? I also wonder if I knew then that *I* was a mestiza, that I was biracial, that I embodied not only a white European side but also, although to a lesser extent, an Indigenous side. I'm not sure at this point. I did not write in a diary my impressions of this day; I never spoke about it as family history with my mother or father. But what I do remember, albeit vaguely, is my seventh-grade teacher's smile of approval, and how I felt clever and original for the first and only time on Halloween.

Part One

THE AGE OF INNOCENCE

The Dragon in the Garden

WHEN I'M SEVEN, HOME IS A suburban mansion on the outskirts of Manila. It has a back garden encircled by a high stone wall covered with vines. Right next door, adjacent to our property but barricaded back by rough rock, is an empty lot left to the mercy of the local flora and fauna. This next-door lot is wild, entangled, its own impenetrable jungle. The rampant vegetation there feels like danger—the inscrutable and forbidden. But even my own more manicured garden holds mysterious dangers. Warned repeatedly by adults about disease-carrying insects, we children constantly watch for white-spotted mosquitoes whenever playing outside on the climbing structure or lawn. "Malaria mosquito! Malaria mosquito!" we shriek, fleeing to the house and the shelter of the indoors.

On one particular day, not unusually, it's muggy and overcast, oppressively humid. My father is at the office, and I'm back home from first grade for the afternoon. My mother and my sister and I join my baby brother and his Filipina nanny upstairs in the nursery. While my mother plays with the baby and my sister and I draw, the nanny, in her starched white uniform, her hair a blunt black bob, folds laundry and entertains us with tales of the Japanese invasion. She tells of families fleeing massacre by walking deep into the rainforest and digging holes under bamboo trees to hide for weeks that turn into months. Of eating rodents and insects. Of capture, torture, devastation, and death. Although I listen, intrigued, and will remember the nanny's words, I don't quite understand them. I only know that I feel anxious. The sadness and the cruelty in these stories are new to me.

Later that afternoon, I run downstairs to fetch more drawing materials, and it is then, as I glance out the window, that I see it: Huge, at least a full meter long. Its clawed feet, its bowed legs, its tail and torso and throat, massive. It's a snake, a lizard—a dragon. As I watch, paralyzed, paper and crayons clutched in my hands, the creature creeps up the shrine to the Virgin Mother, reaching first the bare feet and the carved folds of the gown, then the outstretched arms and the enigmatically smiling face, and finally the modestly veiled head. At last, still staring, transfixed by a sort of terrified fascination, I see the thick tail slide—*slither*—over the wall and disappear into the wilderness next door.

I can't know it in this moment, but the dragon in the garden, the monster in my own backyard, will come to embody for me the ugly side of human nature that is ever-present—even in places supposed to be safe, even in relationships supposed to be innocent.

One night we have a guest over, a colleague of my father's, who is American like us and working for a couple of years in Manila before returning home to the States. Our guest has arrived for the evening with his wife and two adopted boys, the older one around seven, my age. Contrary to what I'll later be accustomed to seeing—US couples adopting children from all over the globe, Chile, China, Ethiopia, Haiti—these boys are American and, what really strikes me, white, whiter than their adoptive parents, flaxen blonds with see-through eyes and pale lashes.

I'm eager with anticipation because we rarely host dinner parties, even in the Philippines, where we have two live-in maids, as well as a baby nurse, chauffeur, and gardener for a house so gratuitously large that five of the rooms upstairs are left permanently closed off, cavernous and musty. Service is cheap, and the American company for which my father and his colleague work pays for all our expenses. To add to my excitement, my mother has given me a ring to wear for the night, a ring with a single perfect pearl, as precious in my eyes as treasure from a bygone era of sultanas and queens. The pearl is so white and lustrous, so completely sufficient in and of itself, so lucent and gleaming, that I can't help but glance down every few minutes to admire its beauty on my stubby finger.

Downstairs, the adults gather in the living room for cocktails, hors d'oeuvres, and small talk. I approach the sofa where the wife sits with her legs properly crossed and her helmetlike hair, back-combed and smoothed over, sprayed into submission. Leaning against the side of the sofa, I place my hands on the arm, ostensibly to support my weight but in reality to display the pearl ring to the fullest advantage. I hover, my eyes fixed on the wife, willing the sophisticated adult to notice my ring.

Finally, my efforts pay off. "Oh my!" the guest exclaims. "That *is* a pretty ring!"

I beam at the nice lady, lifting my hand to allow her to admire the pearl more closely. Then, satisfied, I leave the adults in search of the boys.

AT ONE POINT IN THE YEARS my family spends in the Philippines, we embark on a road trip with my father's colleague and his wife and sons. We leave the city of Manila in three cars and very soon, almost immediately, are driving on roads barely free of swamp and jungle, dark mountains threatening to close in on us from every side.

Early in the trip, I find myself a passenger in the wide sedan driven by the colleague, his wife next to him. I'm alone with the older son in the back seat. It's exciting to drive with parents who are not my own. To be the lone representative of my family. To exchange information with a boy, a boy my own age, until recently unknown to me. I absorb his difference, his strangeness, his utter whiteness. I am brown, a mixture of Anglo and Latino—or, as was more commonly said then, Hispanic. My hair is long, a thick dark black, like the hair of the maids, of most of the girls in Manila. The boy sitting next to me in the car speeding down a road that cuts through dense tropical growth is, to me, different. Other. His crew cut looks bleached, his skin translucent, his eyes shallow pools rather than deep wells. At one point, we position our forearms side by side and compare the different shades. I'm curious about him, as he is about me. We talk about our birthdays, our favorite foods. I think I know what adoption means, but am too shy to ask. Inspired by the attention, by the complicity of sharing the private and the personal, the boy reaches into a bag at his feet and lifts out a glass bottle of pills. "Look! This's my brother's medicine. He has to take it every day." His eyes search my face for confirmation of his contribution to our conversation, for appreciation of the insider knowledge he offers me.

Suddenly the mother's hand flashes from the front seat and strikes her son across his face. The slap reverberates in the stunned pause that follows. Time slows, and I watch the boy hide his reddening cheek with one hand, tears in his clear, light eyes. I can still see him, even now, so many years later, looking at me—this time mortified, humiliated. I do nothing, *can* do nothing.

If I could go back in time, I'd wait until the mother's attention returned to the road unfurling in front of the car, then take his free hand, his left hand, the one that had lain next to mine to be compared. At the very least I'd roll my eyes in the direction of the mother to signal my support. Instead I only stare, feeling his misery, scared and embarrassed myself.

Before turning around to face the front again, the mother hisses, "You *never* talk about your brother's medicine with outsiders! *Do you hear?*"

Two days later we've reached a resort deep in the countryside, overlooking a lake. There is a pool, two restaurants, a playground with a squeaky metal seesaw and rusted swings. The architecture is all arches and courtyards, the décor heavy wood and white stucco: the aesthetic legacy of Spanish colonialism. Nature, however, lies just outside, close by, waiting to reclaim its territory with its green vines and drenching rain, not to mention humidity and mold. For a reason I don't remember now, I'm in a deserted dining room with the younger brother. I haven't spent that much time with him, because I consider him a little boy at five years old. Although I don't know what leads up to the push, I do remember being shoved backward, my head hitting the sharp edge of a chair, and finally lying, stunned, among a thicket of wooden legs and table bases.

Soon enough, there are adults. I'm helped up—questions are asked, my head examined. I still see the blood on my fingers after I explore the throbbing spot on my scalp. I still see the mother leading her younger son away with her arm around him, protectively and comfortingly. I still feel the injustice in the lack of consequences for the younger son. In his getting away scot-free. In the difference between a slap in the face and an arm around the shoulder.

Decades later, when we are back in California, I learn from my father that the older son of his colleague in Manila all those years ago is estranged from his adoptive parents. I learn that we both graduated from the same large university, but I never saw him in the throngs of students on campus. I learn that he has broken ties with his family; they only hear of him from time to time, second- or thirdhand.

Still seeing the humiliation in his eyes and remembering his mother's violent antipathy, I'm sad for him. I realize now, as an adult, that the mother favored his younger brother and I wonder why. Was it something about the older boy's personality? Was it the inherent cuteness of the younger boy? Was it something unknown—a mysterious quality in the little one that the mother herself may never have acknowledged? Although I know that as a child the older son was neglected rather than treasured, I want to believe him liberated now. Actually, I want to believe him more than liberated, I want to believe him happy. But, instead, I'm afraid he might always feel forsaken—a flawed trinket rather than the pearly treasure of sultanas and queens.

Sizzler

MY MOTHER IS AWAY AND MY FATHER, left for an evening with his three children at our house in Northern California, decides to take us on a rare restaurant outing. We are as excited as you would expect children would be who only go out to eat once in a great while, maybe only twice a year. As we prepare for our thrilling adventure of dining at Sizzler, one of us, maybe my brother, misbehaves in some way offensive to my father. He might have refused to tie his shoes properly or put away some toys; perhaps he didn't help in the garden with a small chore when asked. In any case, my father puts his foot down. The offensive child, the one who misbehaved, let's say my brother, will not accompany us to the restaurant in our secondhand sedan with the wide bench seats. He has to stay home, alone, as punishment.

This punishment of my father's is horrifying to all of us. We're used to always having my mother, so warm and affectionate, as a protective and forgiving buffer. A soft flannel blanket of comfort and soothing. Never any of this rough tone of voice, this angry, tough discipline. For us, his punishment feels as harsh as a blow, monumental in its finality, in its exclusion of a child, a sibling, a member of the family. We are aghast.

I don't remember the details of the immediate aftermath, of our wide-eyed absorption of the paternal decree, of crying and begging my father to reconsider, to change his mind, to please, *please* take us all to Sizzler! What I do remember with certainty is my mother's absence, and our joint decision—my sister's and mine—to stay home, to forgo our rare and much-anticipated treat, to be loyal to our brother rather than leave him, alone and bewildered, behind.

Where was my mother? She hardly ever left us when we were children. I doubt she was on one of her trips to Peru to visit her relatives there—she always took us with her. Neither was she the type to belong to an organization like a book club or the PTA in the United States, a culture she felt was prejudiced against her as a "Hispanic" with darkish skin and accented English. I can only guess that she was at an anomalous adults-only evening event with her circle of similarly expat Peruvian friends. An event that for some reason was only for women and not for children, because we usually went with her to these kinds of gatherings as well. But her absence really was as rare as a restaurant outing. And looking back, I'm deeply grateful for her continuous presence throughout my childhood. Without her, I believe my father would have been a different father, a more severe father, perhaps what my mother would consider abusive in his behavior with his children.

I grew up with a story my mother told me, over and over, whenever she was reminded of it by situation or conversation. In this story I'm not yet two years old—the first and, at the time, only child of my parents. We sit, my father and mother and I, at a restaurant table in San Francisco, the city where I was born. In a high chair, and apparently full of one-year-old energy, I am very invested in throwing sugar cubes willy-nilly across the tabletop, onto the floor, at my parents. My father admonishes me to stop. I do not. He reaches across the table and slaps my face.

In my mother's retelling, the restaurant becomes hushed. Did it? Or did it do so only when my mother stood and lifted me from the high chair where I was crying? When, hugging me tightly, she told my father that if he ever touched me again she would divorce him? When she, still holding me in her arms, left him in the restaurant alone at the table for three?

I don't know. She might not even know, her story becoming more and more calcified with every time she told it, her memory beginning to build on its successive iterations as soon as the moment was over.

Regardless, I do know that my mother was the protective shield for me as I grew up in a family divided by personality and culture. The extrovert and the introvert, the generous and the frugal, the permissive and the authoritarian. The warm and social versus the cool homebody, the pop music dancer versus the classical music wallflower, the affectionate versus the disciplinary. Then also, always and simultaneously, the third world and the first, the colonized and the colonizer, the brown and the white.

As an adult, I often looked back at my upbringing and thought of it as only good. I had a happy childhood, and I thought having these two polar opposites as parents made me who I am: a normal, blended person. Now I see that yes, I am (at least in my opinion!) a normal, blended person, but also that living in *la frontera* that was my family—the borderlands where cultures continuously clash, where dwellers inhabit a destabilized, in-between space—must have been stressful. The constant negotiation of opposing personalities that were themselves shaped and informed by cultural differences. The siding with the warm, openly loving mother who had, unlike my father, a loose and carefree attitude about deadlines, homework, school attendance, properly cooked meals, and sparkling kitchens.

My mother was never touched in any way other than affectionately by her parents; she was never shouted at or spoken to harshly. She paid this gentle parenting style forward with her own children. So much so that after learning about my best friend's experience with corporal punishment, I would look askance whenever in her house at the wooden spoon sitting in its container with the other kitchen utensils, thinking it bizarre and frightening—*alien*—to have a designated tool with which to hit a child, a supposedly beloved son or daughter, on a regular basis.

Although not a dedicated storyteller like my mother, my father did have a few stories he would recount to me once in a great while. One took place when he was about five and his brother three. They were playing, with their British mother nearby, on a blanket on the floor of their home. For some reason, probably because of a toy, my then five-year-old father shoved his brother. My grandmother wasted no time and immediately slapped her older son's face. My father always wore the same expression when he told this story: a little bemused, a little ashamed, and a little proud. The confusion and the shame and the pride—together they tell their own story of a sensitive child, a vulnerable boy, an older brother to the younger sibling who is the favorite of his mother. It's clear to me now, looking back at the different times I heard my father recall this memory, that this moment in his young childhood had great impact on him. It makes me sorry for my five-year-old father, the boy who had a mother perpetrating a callous and biased form of discipline so different from my own mother's intensely protective love.

My father's mother, my grandmother, was born and bred in Yorkshire, England. I was scared of her. She was acerbic, biting, sure of her own values and traditions. She told us off, her only grandchildren, with clipped, accented tones, cold and mean. I saw, too, how she disdained my Peruvian mother as a daughter-in-law, and it hurt me even before I had words for bias and racism and prejudice. Before I knew the history of British and then—the motherland giving birth to a mini-me in its colonizing tendencies—American imperialism, an imperialism that defined people like my mother, despite their mixed heritage, despite their elite status in their home country, despite their impeccable manners and bilingualism, as the conquered and the dark, as the interlopers.

My father himself had a strict hierarchy of race. In his ranking, Japanese people specifically (my father spent most of the Korean War stationed in Yokohama) and white people in general were near the top, with brown and immigrant people near the bottom. He stayed true to this hierarchy, so problematic to me, until his death, seemingly indifferent to his wife and children being, all four of us, part brown.

My life—my identity and experiences growing up—was bifurcated. Not like an exile's life, not like my mother's, which was split between past and present, between a beloved homeland and the attempted adoption of an alien culture, but between two vastly different, sometimes conflicting cultures—two contrasting ways of being, of thinking, of navigating daily existence.

My weekdays were spent with a mother who gave us everything we asked for that she possibly could. Trips to McDonald's for tiny and affordable soft-serve ice cream cones, days playing hooky from school to go to Loehmann's and buy discount clothes, more than one girlish diary, replete with images of horses or hearts or rainbows and a tiny brass key that fit in the lock of the equally tiny clasp. Later, in high school, new Pappagallo shoes for our field trip to see *La Traviata* at the opera house in San Francisco, my first set of makeup when I was thirteen, the sewing of custom outfits I designed for myself, the use of our single family car whenever I wanted it.

Those weekdays, full of easy warmth and motherly acceptance, of a taken-for-granted maternal generosity, were interrupted every evening by the arrival of my father from work at five thirty. We would scramble to clean the house, tidying scattered toys or magazines or books, putting away dirty dishes to hide the fact that we'd eaten in the living room, turning off the television so he wouldn't realize we'd watched *Sesame Street* or *Mad Max* or *The Magic Flute*. My father's personality was rigid, his parenting regulated. He had a series of rules that we children were never to break in fear of his anger and disappointment, sometimes of his punishments. He was not an unloving father, but he was, very obviously to my young self, stricter, less easygoing, and more authoritative than my mother. Now I know, as an adult, that he was a product of his own upbringing: British American, Protestant, East Coast boarding school.

It's between these two people and their personalities and cultures and styles of parenting that I grew up. It is between this mother and this father that I had to maneuver and react and take sides. Every day. It's between this set of parents that I negotiated and learned and started to develop my personal brand of mestizaje.

La Frontera. The Borderlands. I see now, in my fifties, what I didn't understand consciously for most of my life, even after I went to graduate school and read Cherríe Moraga, Chandra Talpade Mohanty, Sandra Cisneros, Paula Moya, Gloria Anzaldúa—my heroic role models—that my life in the borderlands didn't start after the age of consciousness, in the world outside home and family. It was always there, inside my family, inside me: the push and pull, the conflict and friction, the constant, never-ending negotiation of values and lifestyles and beliefs. And yes, it has shaped me into what I am now. Just in a different way and into a different person than what I once believed, when I was content for so long to think of my past as *simply* happy.

Marriage and Exile

MY GRANDFATHER HAD JUST FINISHED speaking from his seat at the head of the dinner table when my mother pushed her chair back, her face contorting as she started to cry. I sat mutely as she passed me on her way out of the dining room and up the stairs to the guest bedroom. After a minute, though, I—the firstborn daughter and, at nine years old, already the companion and confidante of my mother—couldn't stand it any longer. I pushed my own chair away from the table to run after her, leaving everyone else, my father and little sister and brother, my grandparents and their guests, to finish dinner without us.

It was December, and we spent every Christmas in Bethesda with my father's parents. Christmas and New Year's were taken very seriously by my Anglo-Saxon grandparents: by my grandfather, who was born in New Jersey to parents of Scottish and Irish heritage, and by my grandmother, who was born and bred in England. There was the Douglas fir to be chosen as a family in a snowy field, then cut down by my father with a hatchet. There were the decorations collected over the decades from years lived in England and Germany and France, as well as the United States. There was the crèche on the mantelpiece, and in the back of the refrigerator the fruitcake that had been marinating patiently since late summer. There was the singing of "Auld Lang Syne" in a hand-held circle at midnight every New Year's Eve.

In my memories, my grandparents are always old. My grandfather hunches forward when he stands, and his walk is the shuffle of the elderly. Gray, wiry hairs sprout from his large ears. My grandmother, a slight, bone-thin woman, sports fleshy bags under her hooded eyes, eyes that were once large and dark. Under her chin is a long, skinny wattle that I stare at with fascination and fearfully obsess about inheriting.

My grandparents are also formal. My grandfather dresses every morning in a three-piece suit and leather wingtip shoes. After a breakfast of black tea and raisin bread toast, he retires to his study. There, on an archaic black typewriter, he painstakingly edits the diaries that record his years as a journalist in Europe and an officer in World War II. He types surrounded by an old-fashioned gramophone that plays his favorite operas and shelves that hold books by James Joyce, T.S. Eliot, Henry James, and William Thackeray. My grandmother has precise notions of decorum for her grandchildren that often seem to me as unintelligible as Chaucer's Middle English. She chastises us with a British accent unsoftened by decades of living in the United States for behaviors we have no idea are rude or offensive. We must say *may* when asking permission rather than *can*: "I am sure you *can*," she continually reminds us, "but the question is *may* you?" We should not laugh too loudly during meals or interrupt the adults. We must only accept a single piece from the tantalizing box of chocolates she offers us, and never ask for a second; when the next day I do, having forgotten her instruction overnight, she reprimands me so sharply that I find myself blinking back tears.

That winter night in Bethesda, I found my mother lying on her bed, the only light coming through the open door from the hallway. She was crying but I didn't know why. I also didn't know how to ask her what was wrong. It all seemed so serious, so awful—the interrupted meal, my mother's tears, the darkened room. I sensed only dimly that it had to do with my grandfather. When one of the guests, a kind woman distantly related to my father's family by marriage, followed us upstairs a few minutes later, I discovered why my mother was so upset. In response to the kind guest's gentle queries, my mother sobbed into her pillow, "He called me an outsider! He told me I don't belong!"

WHEN I WAS A CHILD, I FLEW with my mother, sister, and brother to Lima every year. The plan, according to my father at least, was that we would stay in Peru for three weeks out of our school vacations to give my mother a chance to visit her family before she had to commit to another year in the cold, inhospitable culture of the United States. Invariably, my mother would make a long-distance phone call to my father toward the end of the agreed-upon three weeks to tell him that we needed to stay another week. That week would often stretch to two or three.

Like an addict, my mother craved Peru. She craved spending time with her mother and sister, and speaking Spanish. She craved the hot days, the spontaneous lunches, the afternoons at the country club or long days at the beach, the *ceviche* and the *chicha morada*. She missed, like an amputated limb, the warmth and ease of being in South America, never minding the poverty and the beggars, the dust and dirt, the pickpockets, the electrical blackouts, or even, for a decade or so, the terrorism of the Sendero Luminoso.

My mother's father died when she was seventeen. He left behind a wife sixteen years his junior who mourned him so deeply that she was housebound for a year. He left behind an eldest daughter already two years into her marriage to the love of her life and settled in a hacienda hours outside of Lima. And he left behind my mother, his younger daughter, who had to curtail her own grief to take care of my grandmother and put aside her dreams of studying piano in a musical conservatory to find work. Even so, when she reminisces about this time, my mother doesn't sound sad. She long ago left behind the knife-turning pain of raw grief and now has only a faded regret that her father died when his family was so young. She talks about her life after high school with a cheerful nostalgia, telling me about working as a secretary for Pan American Airlines, a job that afforded her not one but two free around-the-world trips, experiences she treasures to this day. When she wasn't traveling, she spent weekends by the ocean with friends and attended parties with music and laughter and dancing.

There was, however, one major problem — not for my mother but for my grandmother. It bothered her that her daughter wasn't married. That she didn't have a serious boyfriend. That, at the age of twenty-two and then twenty-three, she was getting older and in danger of becoming *una solterona*. In my grandmother's world, being an old maid was not a fate worse than death, but it was definitely worse than marital dissatisfaction or even divorce. Thus it became my grandmother's mission to get my mother married.

There had been candidates before: a doctor twice my mother's age whom she had met on the beach when a teenager, and an architectural student my mother's age whom my grandmother had selected as suitable. The first my grandmother rejected, most probably because of his age, and maybe because her daughter had met him without premeditation or ceremony, without the necessary parental vetting and approval. The second my mother rejected — ultimately, she says, because he was too effeminate for her; she needed someone more masculine. Perhaps she missed the maturity of her first love.

It was that first love, the doctor with whom she walked on the sand and looked at the sunset, who was my mother's true love. When she bowed to her mother's pressure to break it off—it was too inappropriate, he was too old—she was also breaking her own heart.

As a single woman, my mother lived with her mother. Lima's beaches and boardwalks, her high school group of friends who had attended the Sagrado Corazon together and shared memories of first periods, first crushes, and first dances, and her family of sister and mother, of cousins and aunts and uncles, of nephews and nieces, all meant home to her. Until. Until my grandmother decided that that life was not good enough for her daughter. Until my grandmother wanted her to have her own home with a husband and children. *"Pero, Mami,"* said my mother, *"a mi me gusta mi vida como es. Quiero quedarme contigo."* Happy with her life in Lima, my mother wanted to stay with her mother indefinitely, living in the same house, sharing meals and conversations and domestic routines.

"¡A no!" was my grandmother's response. *"¡Eso sí que no! Yo no voy a ser responsable porque nunca te cases."* She wanted her daughter to go to Washington, DC, instead and stay for a while with a cousin who lived there. So my mother left, packed off by my grandmother, to the golden land of opportunity to seek her fortune in the shape of a husband.

Expatriates, even if we think beyond the Steins and the Hemingways and the Fitzgeralds, are different from exiles. The difference is choice. Ah, one might argue, but my mother had choice. She *chose* to marry an American and emigrate to the States. Well, now we are entering the territory of borders and boundaries. Ones that aren't physical like a wall or a checkpoint or a line on a map, but ones that are real nonetheless. Borders that mothers draw around their daughters, boundaries that, to be good daughters, they must respect as if law.

Did my mother have a choice? She was not a political refugee, forced to flee her homeland in order to save her life. She was not an economic refugee, emigrating to the United States because she and her family lacked opportunities for education and advancement in her homeland. She was not an environmental refugee, driven from her country because of destruction wrought by natural disaster: a flood, a tornado, a famine, an earthquake. Yet she was forced, in a way, to leave her beloved Peru. To leave her sister and mother, her work and friends, her house and home.

The pressure of a strong-willed, opinionated mother on a quiet, dutiful daughter can act with the force of a tsunami, gathering strength beneath the surface, unseen, only to push relentlessly when it crests. My mother could not resist her mother's will, her mother's belief that she would lead an impoverished life if single and childless, or her plan to make her daughter marry, even at the cost of leaving her family and her country, even at the price of exile.

My mother moved to the United States, found a job, a group of Peruvian friends, a husband. When at the altar she vowed to marry my American father 'til death did they part, she promised to leave her homeland, to relocate forever, to become an exile. Again, not an exile as in a refugee from political threat, poverty, or disaster. Rather, an exile who was pushed out of her birth country and into a nation foreign to her by her mother's version of the American Dream. In the United States, my grandmother reasoned, her daughter was bound to find a man she liked well enough to marry, as it seemed that in their small Limenean community there was no one who satisfied her. If the problem was her daughter's pickiness, then casting a wider net in a sea that had many more eligible fish might solve it.

But did my mother's success in living that particular version of the American Dream translate into happiness? The cost of a marriage to an eligible bachelor—tall, dark, and handsome, ambitious and intelligent—was loss. Loss of family and community and culture. Loss of home.

Once, when I was somewhere between ten and twelve, old enough to notice things yet still young enough to be confused by them—sometime during the four years we lived in Ecuador—my aunt called to tell my mother that she and my uncle were going to swing by our home in Quito for a few days as part of a longer trip to Miami.

This was a big deal to my mother. She felt so removed from Peru with her permanent home all the way up in Northern California and in a different time zone—not even in Miami, a city that felt almost next door to Peru with its nonstop flights to Lima and its neighborhoods and malls where Spanish was more common than English. And although we were living at that time in Ecuador, which is right next to Peru, we still only visited Lima once a year, probably because of school schedules and my father's reluctance to have his family decamp too often without him. So my mother began to prepare for the coming of her sister and brother-in-law.

It felt to me like the Queen of England was coming to visit, or perhaps the pope. It felt even more special because my aunt rarely visited us; regardless of where we lived, we always went to her. With only twenty-four hours' notice, my mother rushed about the house, washing and cleaning and preparing a bedroom. At one point, as I passed from the living room to the kitchen, I saw her on the stairs. She had been busily vacuuming when the phone rang. It was her sister. She wasn't coming. They couldn't make it after all. My mother sat on a step, the vacuum beside her, the phone with its long cord still in her hand. She was weeping.

My mother held on to her Peruvian citizenship as if it were a treasure; she held it close to her heart as if it were a magic crystal or a golden ticket. She would not give it up. For twenty-six years, although her home base was the United States, she refused to become a US citizen. Her Peruvian passport was like a lifeline to her identity, to her past, to her home. It was like an umbilical cord or an anchor, keeping her tethered to her true self.

Growing up, I flew with my family in and out of the United States at least ten times. Outside of the United States we must have gone through customs at least another ten times as we traveled to Peru, Japan, Colombia, and the Bahamas and lived temporarily in the Philippines and Ecuador. Each time, my mother had to separate from us, from her husband and her small children, to have her passport stamped at a separate kiosk, by a different official. For me, returning from abroad through JFK or MIA or SFO, that meant watching my mother walk away from us to join another line—a much longer line than our quick and efficient queue, the one that seemed bright and cheerful, that seemed to say, *Welcome back, you belong*. My mother's customs line seemed shrouded in a kind of shame, a pall that took its shape and shade from the browner skin within it, the extended time it took, and the more suspicious attitudes of the officials tending it. It seemed to say, *You are Other, you do not belong*. Yet that temporary separation from her family, with its extra hassles and wasted time, was worth it for my mother. It meant that she was still Peruvian, that she still belonged to the country where she'd grown up and to the culture that had formed her.

Some years ago, in 2016, my mother was involved in a minor car accident. I wasn't there, but my son was. My mother had just pulled away from her parking spot in front of my children's middle school with my son beside her when an SUV crashed into the side of her Prius.

My mother loves her grandchildren; she adores them. Her devotion manifests itself through small and continuous acts of service. Even though I don't work, she has always jumped at the chance to take my sons to their piano lessons, to pick them up from school, to sit with them during the evenings when my husband and I want to go on a date night, or to buy them bagels—first calling to get their separate orders, then driving to the deli and standing in line to purchase the bagels, then finally hand-delivering them to our house.

The day of the accident, my son watched as the driver of the SUV, a blonde, ponytailed mother in spandex yoga pants, blamed his grandmother. The policeman who appeared to assess the situation talked to both of the drivers: "I need to see your driver's license," he said to the blonde woman. Then, turning to my mother, the older woman with the brown skin and the Spanish accent, he said, "And I need to see your Social Security card."

"Social Security card?" repeated my mother, confused. "But I have never been asked for my Social Security card by a policeman." She managed to recite her Social Security number from memory, but came home still wondering and distressed, like a child who has been punished without knowing why, about the policeman's unusual request.

My mother was left bearing the stigma of the Other so familiar to the exile—the disorientation of an unnamed shame alongside the anger that has no outlet.

LONG AGO I WATCHED MY MOTHER cry as she lay prone on a bed, her face buried in a pillow. And why was that? Because her father-in-law, my grandfather, had made a comment that excluded her, that highlighted her identity—darker, accented, and South American—as Other. She did not belong. She did not belong in his family, in his country, in his culture. As he was old-school and formal, with a mindset calcified in the 1940s, he probably didn't mean to offend, or to hurt. My mother, after all, *was* different from him—in race and customs, in language and citizenship. Thus he may have been speaking a truth as he saw it at the time.

Yet. Yet it did offend. It did hurt. It hurt so much that it drove my mother from the dinner table, from the group of family and friends come together during the holiday season to celebrate life and community and the advent of a new year; it drove her to seclude herself somewhere away from him, up the stairs, on another floor, in a dark room, unwittingly mimicking the experience of being excluded in her host nation, her adopted culture, her second home.

Today my mother is in her mid-eighties, and in recent years I've noticed a shift in her attitude toward the United States as her residence and toward Peru as her home. She has lost some of that drive that she had for decades to *be* in Lima, to live that life, to breathe that air. She is more content in between visits to Peru, and needs to visit less often. It may have to do with technology and the facility of communication through email, cell phone, and FaceTime. She talks to her sister several times a day, and they show each other on their phones whatever is happening around them: tea on the patio at my house, dinner in the courtyard at my aunt's, a grandson playing the piano in California, the redecoration of a living room in Lima.

Only lately has my mother changed her mind about dying in Peru, about living out her last years with her sister and being cared for by maids and servants known to the family. The other day she told me that when she gets *demasiado viejita*, too old to live independently, I should hire a warm Latina woman to live with her in her own house, someone who speaks Spanish, who is nurturing of manner and relaxed of attitude with that South American ease, who will make sure she is cared for and happy.

What does this say about the experience of exile? About the feelings of the exile? Some might see it as a kind of defeat, but it makes sense for my mother. She is tired. She doesn't want to move to Lima at this age with all the attending upheaval and stress. She also doesn't want to miss seeing her children and grandchildren on a daily basis. But if it is a defeat, it is one that doesn't hurt. The stage of withdrawal is over and done. Although it is a concession, it isn't a relinquishing of her love for her Limenean culture. It isn't a surrender of her Peruvian identity, rather, it is a product of time and age.

Through my mother I have seen firsthand the bifurcation of the exile's identity—in between homes and cultures, but not entirely of either, always inhabiting an uncomfortable limbo, a liminal space defined by sacrifice and loss. Yet. Yet now, so late in her life, in the last eighth, ninth, tenth of her time here on this earth, my mother has finally begun to feel at home where she has put down roots, albeit reluctantly, here in the United States. And we, her children, are her roots. We are the ties that bind, but also the anchors that steady. Perhaps in this way there's been, finally, a move toward completeness.

The Raffle Prize Winner

MY MOTHER STOOD FROM HER PLACE at the table and approached the low stage, taken off guard but pleased nonetheless. They had called her name. From those of hundreds of ladies who lunch, her ticket number had been chosen. She had won the raffle. She later said, *Nunca me toca nada*—I never win anything. She had been singled out, and she was delighted.

Whenever my family lived abroad—in Manila or Quito or Rio—my mother joined a women's group, usually made up of a mix of expats and locals. On the day she won the raffle, she sat at one of the many round tables elegantly set with lavish bouquets of roses, Ecuador's premier luxury commodity, at a fundraising luncheon put on by Quito's women's club. At the podium, the president of Las Damas Latinas handed my mother her prize: a tall, elegant vase, cut-crystal and heavy, its pattern of soft purples and lavenders complementing the silk of my mother's royal-blue dress.

I too was delighted when my mother told me the story of her good fortune after I came home from school that afternoon. How lucky she was! She won a prize! And one so beautiful and precious! I held the vase carefully in both hands, appreciating the exquisite pattern of amethyst diamonds carved into the thick crystal. It seemed to my eleven-year-old eyes a treasure worthy of Ali Baba's cave.

For long afterward we associated the raffle prize with good luck, with felicitous coincidence and favorable chance. It gave me a feeling of storybook magic whenever I looked at it in its place of honor on the table in our living room, as if it had been conjured from a fairy godmother's wand.

It was many months, perhaps a year later that we learned that contrary to what we believed, my mother's raffle win had nothing to do with luck or fortune, and everything to do with a family holiday taken weeks before.

OUR ROAD TRIP TO COLOMBIA FROM Ecuador was the only one my family took during our four years living in Quito. We had a small station wagon just big enough to fit our suitcases in the rear, my two younger siblings and me in the back seat, and my parents up front.

It took us an entire day to arrive at our destination after an early morning start. I don't remember much about the drive, only the disappointedly rainy days of our Colombian stay. We were at a resort, that much I know, with a pool and a lake, but it was hard to take advantage of these amenities in the damp of the pseudo-tropics. Neither do I remember much about what we actually did to amuse ourselves as children when it was too wet to spend time outside. I assume my father read his newspapers contentedly between meals. I'm sure he made us go on at least one walk a day, as he always did wherever we were, rain or shine. Do I remember rubber boots wading through the mist at the edge of a dark silent lake? Or breakfasts in an airy white dining room with a view of the watery green world outside? I think I do, but rather than clear recollections sharply delineated, these memories are faded photographs rendered blurry and indistinct by time.

Nor do I remember much about our drive back to Quito,

with the exception of one incident: soldiers stopping our car at the border and refusing my mother reentry into Ecuador. I remember quick conversations between my parents; I remember a decision being made for my mother to stay there, at the checkpoint, with her purse and her passport, and for the rest of us to continue on so that my father could go to work and we children could go to school the following day.

Thinking back, it's striking to me that I wasn't more afraid of leaving my mother behind. I am the oldest daughter and she and I were very close. Why wasn't I more worried? Maybe because back then, at the age of ten or eleven, I had no real knowledge of politics, border controls, or citizenship laws. My parents probably made light of the situation in front of their children, not wanting to worry us or make traumatic the parting at the military kiosk.

Over the next few years I gradually put together, in the vague, hazy, piecemeal way that children do, a narrative around that moment at the border that acted as a wall barring my mother from leaving one country and entering another. There had been a flare-up that year in the generations-old border dispute between Ecuador and Peru. As can happen with land grabs and power struggles, there existed a geopolitical limbo between the two feuding nations, both claiming on official maps the in-between territory at the border for themselves. It began with reports of shots fired by soldiers stationed there. Subsequently from the news we learned about protests in each country demonizing the citizens of the other: Peruvians tying monkeys (representing Ecuadorians) and Ecuadorians tying chickens (representing Peruvians) to the ends of sticks, the better to brandish them aloft and swing them about as they chanted xenophobic insults.

How did this affect my family? My mother's passport, her official identity, her citizenship, were all Peruvian. She had asked us during this time of political friction to refrain from talking about her nationality with others, fearing being singled out by Ecuadorians as the enemy.

As we attempted that day to return to our home in Quito, the soldiers at the border held my Peruvian mother hostage, denying her access to Ecuadorian territory. I know now, after having heard the story repeatedly over the years during which I became more aware of political affairs and international conflicts, that my mother was frightened that day at the border, still in Colombia, not allowed to set foot in Ecuador. The mother of three young children, left without husband or family, she felt stranded in that in-between space, alone and in a precarious position, without recourse or agency; she felt unmoored, with no inviolate identity to anchor her, to secure her to the protection of the citizenship she needed at that moment. There was no United States embassy across the way, like a genie in a lamp to magic her to safety. But my father, perhaps complacent in his solid American identity and insensitive to the vulnerability my mother felt, was nothing if not pragmatic—he needed to get home for work, the children needed to get home for school, his wife would have to sort things out on her own and catch up with us later.

And that is what she did, eventually. She had to stay for hours, if not overnight, sitting in the kiosk, making calls to different agencies. Ultimately, the soldiers received orders from some higher authority to let her go and she was allowed, since there was no train station or airport or car service, to board a bus bound for Quito.

This bus was full of a variety of travelers: men and women and at least one young boy, farmers and peddlers and small business owners. My mother was the only person of affluence. She was taller, more expensively dressed, her hair salon-styled; she wore fine leather shoes and sported a designer purse. It would have been clear at a glance that she was different—a fact that proved fortunate for her.

A couple of hours into the trip, the busload of passengers was stopped by a group of military police. This time they were not interested in ascertaining nationalities, but instead in fleecing the travelers of money and valuables. After they were forcibly disembarked from the bus, the peasants and farmers and peddlers emptied their pockets in the face of the machine guns pointed directly at them. One by one, they gave up the little cash they had as my mother watched through the window from her seat on the bus.

My mother was not harassed in any way. The soldiers left the only upper-class woman alone, fearing future retribution from a rich husband or family, or from political connections. The solitary boy on his way back home from the market, however, had the few *sucres* he'd earned in exchange for his family's produce stolen from him in a matter of seconds.

My mother recounts the almost physical pain she felt watching this little boy realize the small tragedy that had befallen his family and run after the police jeep, crying for his money. *¡Qué pena me dió!* When he was forced to give up and returned to the bus, his face grimy with dust and tears, his chest heaving with sobs, she felt compelled to give him all the cash she had on her. Emptying her pocketbook, she handed a bundle of bills to the boy. This more than compensated for the money he had lost to the soldiers. He revived instantaneously, his spirits rising like a wilted flower that has finally been watered, and smiles wreathed his still-wet cheeks.

My mother's trials were not yet over, however. A few hours further into their journey, when she was thoroughly hungry and thirsty, hot and fatigued from her long ordeal, the bus stopped at a junction where food and drinks were sold to weary travelers.

A few of the passengers brought out coins they had managed to squirrel away somewhere on their persons, hidden from the eyes of the police who had sought to steal everything they had. The little boy happily took out the sucres my mother had gifted him and bought an ice-cold bottle of Coca-Cola and an empanada, which he drank and ate enthusiastically, seemingly without a care in the world. My mother, thirst parching her throat, hunger digging into her stomach, could only watch as the boy enjoyed his meal, innocently unconscious of the need my mother felt for a tiny portion of the money she had given away, or for just a bite and a sip of his bounty.

SHE SURVIVED, AS THEY SAY, to tell the tale. It is a story she has told her children many times. In the way of family stories, it evolved into one of our legends, a heroic tale of perseverance—but also a cautionary one, warning of fortune's fickle nature.

My mother finally did become a US citizen three years after we left Ecuador and returned to California. We went as a family to San Francisco's Civic Center, where she took part in a ceremony with a large group of people from all over the world who together swore allegiance to the flag of the United States of America. Afterward, amidst the families congratulating each other, I saw a little boy with black hair and a round face squatting on the sidewalk—comfortable, bored, unconcerned. Although I didn't right then, I wonder now where the other little boy is these days. The little boy on the bus in Ecuador who didn't have the luxury of boredom or comfort or relaxation. I wonder if he is alive or dead. Did he die of disease or accident or violence? If he is alive, I imagine different scenarios: Perhaps he left his parents' home as soon as he was able, traveled to a big city, and found some kind of employment there—working at a market, gardening in fancy neighborhoods, repairing cars as a mechanic; possibly he left home and got married, setting up his own small business in a neighboring *pueblo*; or he may have elected to stay home, helping his parents in their old age, bringing a wife into the fold, having children, inheriting the farm.

In my parents' house down the street from my own, my mother still has the raffle prize from the Damas Latinas luncheon so many years ago. The heavy crystal vase sits, among other cherished objects, on a special shelf. We know now what we didn't know that happy day my mother's name and ticket number were announced from the stage—that certain members of her women's group had heard of my mother's ordeal at the border, and that the Colombians among them had determined to try to make up for her suffering. They had carefully planned the whole raffle by planting the first-prize ticket and thus ensuring that my mother was singled out as the winner.

The moral of this story is still not clear to me, probably because there is actually more than one, but I believe it has to do with identity, with time and place and culture, with imperialism, politics, and nationalism, with the shifting and relative nature of luck. What I do know for sure is that the vase sits there still, visible to all who visit my mother's home, a talisman against the human impulse to create boundaries and define borders, as well as a reminder of people's capacity for empathy, of their instinct to help and desire to set things right.

Stomach Contents

AT TWELVE YEARS OLD, I SAT ON a wooden piano bench, in a small enclosed music room, alone with my elderly teacher and listened as she told me a story.

It may have been during a brief interlude in the lesson, like a mini-intermission, that I stopped picking my way through a piece to turn my eyes from the sheet music and toward my teacher, my hands dropping to my lap. It could have been for a short break that she paused in her modeling of different finger positions with soft, wrinkled hands or ceased to point out the nuances in the chords with a single digit (its nail trimmed blunt, the better to play the piano with). Or perhaps it was during that lingering time at the end of a lesson, after I'd collected my piano books but before I'd gotten up from the wooden bench, when there were sometimes a few minutes left over to talk about things other than notes and fingering and technique.

At whatever moment, before or in between or after the actual lesson, my teacher—an older woman, a wife, mother, and grandmother—chose me, a young girl, a student, middle schooler, and beginning piano player, to tell her tragic tale to. But . . . there remains a pressing question. *Why?* Looking back over the span of years and decades, of adulthood and motherhood, I see that the telling of this story was inappropriate—ill-advised, mistaken, just plain wrong.

What do I make of it now, this sharing of an adult story, this confession of a too-mature situation? I realize that with no guide and no experience I was a slate so blank it was a gamble as to what would, in any lasting way, imprint on my psyche. I had no idea then what to make of the actual story—the situation, the plot, the climax—or the act of its sharing. I did feel special, and somewhat proud, to be the recipient of this beloved teacher's confidence, not realizing, at least not consciously, its tactless nature. I know what I was then—young, immature, innocent, eager to please, desperate for knowledge and experience; and what I felt—honored to have been chosen by a respected adult as a confidante, gratified to have been singled out as a sort of secret-keeper; and finally, what I appeared to be—a pubescent girl with limbs too long, face too thin, ears and front teeth protruding, serious and awkward and earnest. Yet I was chosen by this teacher, this mother grieving what happened to her daughter, to hear her tale, as if a priest in a confession box who in the listening has the power to absolve the sin and lift the burden of sorrow.

But I wasn't a priest; I wasn't wearing the vestments of the confessor; I wasn't sitting in the shadows sheltered by dusty drapes parted only to expose a protective screen. I wasn't even a teenager, let alone an adult. Perhaps it was my purity as an innocent that drew this confession from my teacher. In any case, she wasn't Catholic, as I was; instead she taught at a missionary school that required—insisted on—evangelical beliefs in its faculty. It could be that this was one of the invisible and unarticulated reasons why she felt the need to unburden herself of her daughter's tribulations by saying them out loud to another, to someone so young and trusting and deferential that there could be no danger of interruption, condemnation, or disbelief. Whatever her motivation, with the two of us sitting at the piano as if with an old friend, cocooned by familiar protective walls, safe and sheltered, this worried mother, this teacher and guide to the innocent and the inexperienced, became finally emboldened to speak what had seemed unspeakable.

What did happen in this story? What was said? What constituted this confidence received by a young girl in a small closed room, sitting at an old upright piano, its keys worn, its wooden frame scratched and faded, alongside her kindly older teacher?

IN THE MUSIC ROOM ALMOST EXACTLY forty-two years ago, I looked at my teacher's lined, careworn face and listened to the soft tones of her strange tale as she worried her plain wedding band with spotted fingers. The few concrete bits and pieces remaining of the rubble of the initial foundation of that story told long ago: A grown-up daughter back in the States. Married. A young wife, a young husband, a first home. Where, exactly? Texas? Ohio? Minnesota? I may never have been told that detail, and so there may be nothing to have forgotten.

I still assume now what I took for granted then, that this beloved daughter and young wife grew up Christian in the evangelical, born-again style. The kind of Christian that is baptized after the onset of the age of reason, as an adolescent instead of shortly after birth as I was. A commitment freely chosen, a faith consciously embraced. Jesus Christ would be her Personal Savior; there would be no need for a go-between to mediate problems and translate petitions. On the day of her wedding, she would have earned her white dress.

Back to the concrete: the young husband again, this time fallen on the floor, the framed photo of the newly married couple, smiles innocent, looking down from the mantlepiece.

Dead of unknown causes. I always imagine him slight of build and dark-haired. He could have been big and buffed and blond; yet after all these years, the image of muscles straining a T-shirt, of light, cropped hair instead of soft brown, doesn't fit for me. Either way, he is alone in the house. Either way, there is the evidence.

These days this particular narrative of my past is couched in darkness. All I can see is the teacher telling me her story, and within that one, another—the story itself. The specifics have faded, and the heart of the story has been completed only with the passage of years and the maturity that comes with it.

Because I was too young and inexperienced to have been exposed to certain behaviors around sexuality, I don't have a clear recollection of what exact words my piano teacher used to describe the root of her grief. I only have vague images, I'm sure sketched in with details over time as I learned more about sex. Yet to this day the images remain hazy, their outlines blurred. There is the fallen body, the young man collapsed. There is some kind of autopsy, some kind of discovery. And then there is what they, the doctors and the pathologists and the forensic authorities, eventually report: semen.

Maybe Veronica Clark would have known what was going on—what the words falling from the piano teacher's lips, soft-spoken yet precisely enunciated, meant. Veronica was one of those all-knowing girls, precocious for a middle schooler in those more innocent times, who could critique with sophistication other, less knowing and not-yet-as-mature girls' missteps and blunders. She always called me out on my insecurities, sometimes mockingly, sometimes kindly, telling me what I should have said or done or even thought. This is the reason, I'm sure, that I remember her name so well, even into my mid-fifties. So maybe Veronica Clark would have known about the events implied in my teacher's story.

I had no concept of fellatio whatsoever until, two years after my family had returned to California and I'd stopped taking piano lessons, I heard the term "blow job" for the first time as a sophomore in my Catholic high school. Sitting at my desk in a classroom filled with uniformed girls, a cross on the wall and the Virgin outside in the garden, I giggled helplessly with my best friend in disgusted disbelief—how could such an act exist?

This is the tragic culmination of my piano teacher's tale, the cause of her grief, the pain she held for her daughter and the destruction of her daughter's life: sperm in the belly. I can't imagine today what words she used that afternoon in the music room to convey this idea to me, this surreal, fantastical fact.

To say I was a sheltered child is a gross understatement. I grew up under the watchful eye of an overprotective mother, rarely apart from her, physically or emotionally. She never once shouted at me; she never once punished me; she was instead patient and loving and affectionate. We, my brother and sister and I, were like cherished extensions of her very self. For the fifth, sixth, seventh, and eighth grades I attended a small missionary school in Quito founded to board the children of those called to testify and bear witness in the heart of the South American rainforest. This school was kind and gentle. We had Bible lessons, and we prayed at assemblies, in class, and at various events, from regular meetings to baptisms and graduations. Cursing was never heard. Because "taking the Lord's name in vain" was frowned upon, we never said, *Oh my God!* or *Jesus Christ!* The adults never said, *For God's sake* or *God forbid* or *Oh my Lord*. The six-inch rule forbade kissing or cuddling between boyfriend and girlfriend. Abstinence was the only option in regards to premarital sex. I'd never heard of abortion; divorce was maybe whispered about. Did I know what homosexuality was? Did I ever hear the word "gay" used to describe someone as other than lighthearted? I don't think I knew the words "semen" or "sperm" or "spunk." In fourth grade, before we moved from California to Quito, I asked a classmate what "fuck" (the word I'd seen graffitied somewhere) meant, and in that way found out the facts of life. So I knew the rudimentary outline of the sex act, and that that was the way babies were made, but I definitely was not aware of any of its recreational offshoots.

Today, a mother myself, someone who has been an educator and taught young people in classrooms, I wonder at the temerity of that elderly piano teacher at a missionary school in the 1970s. Or if not the temerity, then perhaps the desperation. What made her speak? What made her tell that story? Some powerful emotion must have compelled her to do so, because in hindsight it seems an almost abusive act. Although I don't remember trauma around that moment in the music room at a piano lesson, a trusting child alone with a confiding adult, there is violence in such an act: the act of articulating a too-mature story to a still-immature child. Perhaps my very innocence, my concrete ignorance, served as a protective shield for my psyche, keeping me from absorbing the bald facts at a time when such things (fellatio and swallowing, sudden death and autopsies) would seem to me grotesque science fiction, a horror story, monstrous and frightening.

Somehow, some way, my piano teacher communicated to me the naked fundamentals of the truth of what happened. Of what was discovered and the destruction to happiness and faith and the belief in an orderly world that ensued. In time, and through observation, conversation, and reading, I learned enough to be able to assign labels to the nature of the stomach contents and the act that got them there.

I'll never know why she said what she said, for that teacher is long gone—dead for many years now, I'm sure. I don't remember her name, and if I could, would I look her up to discover what happened after she retired from teaching at the missionary school? To find an address for one of her children, perhaps that very daughter who featured in the tragedy of her maternal experience? Would I ever dare to write or email or call to ask for an interview? No. Of course not. Doing so would violate the boundaries of propriety; in doing so I would be mirroring the transgression of privacy and respect that her mother, my teacher, enacted in the first place.

I'll never know either if my teacher told any other student that same story. Was it something she couldn't keep quiet about and, Tourette's-like, found herself blurting out in all its sordid details to anyone who came near? No one else mentioned anything about the piano teacher and her daughter to me. I never mentioned the story to anyone, probably because I wouldn't have known how to begin to articulate the actual events of its mysterious plot. I wonder if it had more to do with myself, the listener, if she saw something in me that encouraged her speech. Perhaps I looked vaguely like her daughter, and something in my face or mannerisms triggered her confession. Or maybe it was the particular moment that contained a confluence of factors, a perfect storm of timing and mood and my standing in for unsullied, still-pure youth. Yet even with my adult perspective, with a hindsight honed by experience and motherhood, I refuse condemnation. In this way I *am* like a priest who once heard a penitent in the confessional. I absolve, I forgive, I believe I understand. I never judged in the first place, not only because I was too young and ignorant but also because I loved my piano teacher. I trusted her patience and her gentleness and her loving investment in me.

A parallel story: During these same middle school years, I took woodshop. It must have been a requirement, for I was neither interested in nor skilled at the mechanics of sawing, sanding, or hammering. For one of my projects, I was inspired to create a wooden sign for my piano teacher's room. I saw it in my imagination hanging proudly from a nail on the door.

I set to work first cutting, with one of those thin bendable saws, a round circle that turned out far from perfect, and then, much harder, and even more imperfect, five capital letters, P-I-A-N-O. Next followed the second set of letters, this time four capitals, R-O-O-M. I glued these awkward letters in the center of the circle before varnishing the whole thing. Looking at it the next day, when the varnish had dried, I judged. I condemned. I relegated my creation to the trash can. It was garbage—ugly, misshapen, a Frankenstein's monster of carved wooden signs.

One day a couple of weeks later, I arrived at the music room ready for my lesson with my piano books tucked in the crook of an arm. With astonishment I gazed at the closed door, even as my free hand reached for the doorknob. There it was, my sign, as I had imagined it before its creation, hanging brazenly from the door in all its imperfection: PIANO ROOM. Someone (the janitor? the woodshop instructor?) had spotted the sign in the trash, fished it out, and presented it to the piano teacher. When I exclaimed my surprise at finding my sign on her door, my teacher was delighted. She had been wondering who thought so much of her that they'd taken the trouble to handcraft a sign for her room.

Perhaps at the end of this story—my story that holds within it the memory of another's tale—it's not the inappropriate narrative, the act of confessing to the wrong person, or the risk of traumatizing the listener that is of paramount importance. Perhaps what counts in the end is the relationship itself—the bond between two people, between adult and child, mentor and protégé, between a teacher and her student.

Part Two

INNOCENCE ERODED

Infidel

MY GRANDFATHER VISITED my family's home in California from his in Bethesda sometime in the late eighties. I still lived with my parents, commuting the half hour to my university on weekdays. Having recently become a widower, my grandfather made the plane journey across the continent alone. Although much had changed for him—his wife of forty-five years was dead, his body beginning to curve forward, his hair thinning and white—he still wore a suit every day: vest, jacket, and tie, with leather wingtip shoes. In a photograph taken during that visit, my grandfather sits on a sofa in our house wearing a gray suit, his hair still just thick enough to brush back in his usual style, stubble bristling on wrinkled cheeks in spots that his razor, guided by hands that now trembled, missed that morning.

Getting older, I'm more and more grateful for these images that help me remember, that often trigger a long-forgotten feeling, an emotion, or even a since-rejected perspective. There are photographs in albums and frames, tucked into books and wallets, and, less reverentially, stuffed into plastic sandwich bags then stored away on garage shelves. As I age past menopause, my memory has changed; like my body, it's no longer supple and strong. Instead, it has become patchy, like the mangy fur of a stray dog in the streets of a South American city. Increasingly, there is blank space and white noise where once were fine strokes, rich colors, layered harmonies. Perhaps it is because of this particular photograph, one now lost but still in my memory, that I retain a certain image of my grandfather. Who can say how much I would remember without it of my grandfather's appearance: his daily uniform, his dignified affect, his serious expression?

This photograph invariably reminds me of a letter my grandfather wrote to my father some time after his visit with us. The image of my grandfather in a certain place at a certain age is associated, forever, with that one letter. I imagine the pages typewritten, full of mistakes and crossings-out and typed-over phrases. My grandfather had been a journalist, and writing in a diary was part of his daily ritual, a diary that melded the public and the political with the personal and the private. I have seen a copy of this diary that spans over twenty years, homes in three countries, and two world wars. It is typed, and has the mistakes and errors of an old-fashioned manual typewriter before correction fluid or, much later, word processing. In this letter one thing stands out, more of a comment than a question: "I understand that an infidel will be joining the family."

Infidel.

At the time I didn't know enough to be offended for my fiancé—the Arab, the Muslim, the "infidel." I didn't think of him in those terms; I didn't pigeonhole him into categories of religion, race, or nationality. Instead I thought of meeting him late into the night at underground clubs to dance to the alternative music we both loved; of being introduced by him to sushi, one of his favorite foods, which since then has become one of mine; of his taking an intensive Spanish class one summer so he could communicate more comfortably with my Peruvian grandmother; of our road trip through Scotland when I was nineteen, driving hours a day around lochs and staying in quaint stone bed-and-breakfasts one cold winter (I wore my thick woolen coat all day, every day). I did sense the judgment coming from my grandfather, typed in black and white, stark and superior, but treated it as a joke, a quirky sentiment, a primitive bias based on outdated notions of ethnicity and religion. And I didn't dwell.

But then my father, in his retirement, started going through the boxes of old photographs and negatives gathered throughout the years and mostly forgotten, digitizing and organizing them roll by roll. He sent the rest of the family a few representative ones every day via email, giving us a date, a place, sometimes an anecdote. This photograph, taken some thirty years ago during my grandfather's visit, never made an appearance, and may never be found, but others of my grandfather and grandmother, of their homes in Berlin and Paris and Bethesda, of various ceremonies and celebrations in their lives, were found, dated, and commented on by my father. It is these that triggered my recollection of that photograph of my grandfather seated on our couch, so close in time to his letter to my father and thus to the memory of that word: *infidel.*

I've therefore been prompted to ponder what allowed me to distance myself from my grandfather's judgment. And I consider myself lucky. The closer in relationship and generation, the more difficult it is to see it from afar: the superiority that was taken for granted. I was much closer to my grandmother on my mother's side—"Mamita," as we all called her—yet she was egregiously racist, and, in her good intentions for her daughters and granddaughters and nieces, also sexist. It must be that I am fortunate she didn't extend her brand of racism to my fiancé, that she in fact adored him. I could continue to love her without the angry, pained conflict that can accompany personally felt prejudice; she didn't drive me to angry passions, as she did my sister.

An example: How delighted was the little brown boy in Peru, dirty and dressed in rags, to clean the car's windshield. How he jumped up over and over, skinny and short, trying to reach the top of the windshield. How my grandmother peered from inside the car and pointed at leftover smudges and smears. How the little boy threw his body over the hood in an effort to reach the section of the glass my grandmother indicated. How my sister, filled with pity for this poor boy, yelled at our grandmother about her meanness and then left the car, slamming the door behind her. How my grandmother looked at me with raised eyebrows that said, *What's up with her?* How I knew exactly what was up with my sister, and also exactly how befuddled my grandmother would remain no matter how hard I tried to explain my sister's outrage at her behavior, at her callous exploitation of another human being—a child, poor and hungry. How I chose not to engage because I knew there was no hope of understanding, of agreement: My grandmother was too old, too set in her ways, too rigid in her internalization of class divisions and status, of the normalcy of her role as boss and the little boy's as a kind of subordinate peon. (In the end the little boy was compensated for his efforts; my sister and I had learned to carry loose cash whenever in Lima, the easier to hand out to those exploited by our Peruvian relatives.)

Thus I consider myself lucky in that my grandmother never exhibited toward my infidel fiancé the kind of prejudice she so casually exhibited toward the poorer, browner people in her own country. What if the infidel-as-insult-wielding relative had been, instead of my alienating Anglo grandfather, my beloved maternal grandmother? A grandmother I had always felt close to, someone I loved talking with, shopping with, contentedly eating ice cream with on a bench overlooking the

San Francisco Bay and the Golden Gate Bridge? How would I have felt? What would I have done?

Again, I was lucky. Her bigotry pointed toward a classed and raced Other and away from my fiancé.

Infidel. Without faith. Nonbeliever. Outsider. That's how I defined the word back when my grandfather first wrote the letter to my father—a letter that may have been intended to be congratulatory, acknowledging my father's news that his daughter was soon to be married, but instead betrayed a habitual Christian snobbery. His generation was one that drew clear lines between Jew and gentile, Christian and infidel. Neither he nor my father were circumcised, thus providing physical evidence of their superior Christianity—not circumcised, thus not Jewish, not Muslim. His prejudice against Jews and those he called Mohammedans was cultural rather than personal, and therefore accepted without question, the distinctions between groups of believers calcified into dogma and regarded as immutable. For much of his life, a marriage between different religions was considered a kind of travesty, as wrong as miscegenation between whites and Blacks. I knew my grandfather well; in the way of younger generations, I recognized his anti-Semitism as old-school and obsolete, a relic of a dying philosophy of life. Although there was a hurtful side to my grandfather's distaste for my fiancé's religion, it didn't feel personal. His judgment was removed from me.

I wonder today, as a wife for thirty-plus years, as a mother of two half-Syrian sons, if there are other definitions of that word, used by my grandfather so long ago to describe the man who became my husband. Muslim, Arab, *infidel*. What does it mean to me now that my grandfather is long dead and I've been married to my infidel for over three decades?

If I think about it, these days *I* might be considered an infidel. I am without faith, anymore, in my great-aunts' Catholicism, with its commitment to daily Mass and its adoration of the priests to whom they willed their house. I am also without faith in my paternal grandparents' stoic and rarely alluded to Presbyterianism. I have long been without faith in the fervent, fairy tale–like Evangelicalism taught me in my missionary middle school. I have always been without faith in my paternal grandfather's and my maternal grandmother's individual forms of racism. This loss and lack of various faiths, this turning of my back on bequeathed familial belief systems, can be understood as betrayal—of family, culture, God.

Thus I suspect that my grandfather, if he could see from beyond the grave and into my head and heart to discover my value system today, with its alien politics and philosophies, might find it all so off-putting that he would now also call me, regardless of granddaughter status, *infidel*.

Underbelly

IN THE RENTAL CAR, my sister and I drive through the gathering darkness from Lisboa to Cascais. Passing a sprawling ghetto on the outskirts of the city, I'm reminded of the projects visible from the highway entering another city, New York. On vacation today in Portugal, with my sister at the wheel of the compact rental, we seem to be passing miles and miles of crumbling concrete buildings, hastily made, cheaply constructed, eroding before their time. Worn underclothes, faded jeans, T-shirts, and diapers hang from clotheslines outside of kitchen windows, vying for space with bulky air conditioners that perch, gargoyle-like, high up in the air.

I think about the toddlers who wear the diapers, and somehow in my mind they're crying, ignored and disconsolate, and then I think about the mothers who wash those diapers, and they are invariably thin and tired. A sense of melancholy spreads over my vision of families living closely in such cramped quarters. But I could be falsely projecting my ignorance—why not imagine a toddler laughing as his mother pauses in her washing or dusting or reading and grabs him to her chest, covering his cheeks with quick, impulsive kisses? Or a family, complete with father, mother, sister, and brother, sitting companionably on the couch sharing a big bowl of potato chips while watching a favorite program?

As I stare out the car window, I see that hundreds of black TV antennas spike the dusky sky, and they suddenly replace the sharp Gothic towers forming the cathedrals that we, as tourists, are meant to admire and associate ever after with Portugal and its history.

Twilight gives way to night as we pass the acres of decrepit apartment complexes to enter a desolate wood. The headlights shine on the pale undersides of the leaves from tree after tree lining the empty highway. At first it feels as if we're the only ones on the road, in the solitude of the darkened forest, but then, from the dim cocoon of the rental's interior, I spot a car parked to the side. A man in a leather jacket steps out of his hatchback. As we drive by, I have time to glimpse the pale face of a young woman, lank-haired and thin, among the bushes and tree trunks. I become aware of more cars, incongruous in this leafy forest, awkwardly parked off the main road. My eyes pick up flashlights, furtive figures, men, girls.

"What's going on?" I ask into the dark warmth dimly lit by the dashboard. "Who're those people?"

"Men come here to have sex—to find *putitas*," responds my sister, her eyes on the road. "Isn't that sick?"

Yes, I agree silently, leaning back into the soft seat of the rental car. It *is* sick—the pale faces, startled and female, momentarily lit up by the high beams before fading back into the dark behind us. The women on the dirt of the forest floor servicing a never-ending stream of needy men. The projects we had just passed that were full of people yet evoked for me, in their unknowability—in my unknowingness—a sense of disconnection and fragmentation.

As we leave the woods, I'm left thinking about my life—replete with washer and dryer and two-car garage, with boxwood hedges and flagstone patios and an electronic gate,

with sushi restaurants and walks around shining reservoirs—
so far away from the lives of the women here among the trees,
so far away from the apartment dwellers, their very existence
unknown to me except in this moment, already over.

Fear

Fear of the Unknown

BEFORE THE TRIP, AS A YOUNG wife three years into my marriage, I anxiously inquire of my in-laws what to expect—mainly, will people in Syria speak English? Although fluent in English and Spanish, I know only a handful of words in Arabic: *tayira* (plane), *sayara* (car), *jibneh* (cheese), *tayeb* (good), *shukran* (thank you), *halal* (lawful), *haram* (forbidden).

"Oh yeah," my brother-in-law casually assures me. "Don't worry, everyone there knows English as well as Arabic."

Okay, phew. Good to know.

Fear of Being Rude

After landing on the runway, we descend from the plane, squinting in the sun, and cross the tarmac to go through customs at the Damascus airport. There we find a group of relatives waiting eagerly for us. In the general flurry of greetings and hugs and back slaps, I receive introductory kisses from the women and handshakes from the men.

Anxious to do the right thing, I approach a middle-aged man I spot hovering at the periphery of the cluster of happy and excited family members. Dressed in basic gray cotton, he contrasts with the rest of the group in their elegant sportswear, and he is the only person worrying a string of plain wooden prayer beads.

Hand outstretched, I smile, awkwardly offering a mumbled "pleased to meet you." Rather than reciprocate my gesture, however, he only nods his acknowledgment while avoiding even the slightest contact by swiftly moving his arms behind his back. Confused and embarrassed, I drop my hand, my tentative smile fading.

Later someone tells me that this uncle belongs to an Islamic sect whose male members do not touch women, on any pretext, at any time, except mothers, wives, and daughters.

Thanks a lot, I think. *Someone could have warned me.*

Fear of Big Brother

Starting with the taxi ride from the airport to the Sheraton Damascus, I see images of Assad Sr. everywhere. He seems to look out from every surface: hanging from rearview mirrors, plastered on huge billboards, painted in state-sponsored murals, perched on the roofs of taxis, displayed prominently, in flocked black velvet, on the interior walls of private homes. His face is ubiquitous, ever watching, like Orwell's Big Brother or the bespectacled eyes of Fitzgerald's Doctor T. J. Eckleburg. I also notice posters, sprinkled here and there, of the eldest son and heir—the one once destined to inherit the presidential throne, the one now dead in a car crash involving 150 miles per hour in a Maserati—smiling in flashy aviator glasses and a military jacket. *It's as if,* people say, *the father wants to pretend he's still alive.*

When I innocently ask from the back of the taxi if women routinely vote in this country, my mother-in-law shushes me, a finger on her lips, casting an anxious glance to the front of the car before whispering, "Don't talk about politics here—you never know who is working for the government." Startled, I stare at the graying head of the mild-mannered driver.

After the taxi deposits us at the hotel, my husband and I settle in our room, luxurious in its décor of brass lamps, walnut furniture inlaid with mother-of-pearl, and wall panels carved with configurations traced in silver and sage. I soon discover that through room service I can order *mahalabia,* the delicious custard my father-in-law makes regularly at home. As the cool pudding, subtly sweet with milk, sugar, and rose water, lingers on my tongue, I gaze out the large picture window from the settee where I sit and see, situated high on the arid brown mountain opposite the hotel, the presidential palace—a marble fortress, really, a massive monument to totalitarian power that seems intentionally positioned to intimidate the population below. Dominating the broad plateau on Mount Mezzeh, the palace is huge, a white block radiating the glare of the sun, protected from enemies by slabs of concrete, security walls, and opaque black windows.

Fear of Being Left Out

I sit on a low, wide sofa. Thick velvet drapes muffle the honking of cars and the calls of street vendors while shielding the room from the heat of the summer. Silk Persian rugs cover the floor, wall to wall, soft under bare feet. The family has gathered at an aunt's house for lunch in the late afternoon. After eating, we've assembled in the salon, where we sip, from small delicate glasses, hot black tea oversweetened with heaping spoonfuls of sugar. All around are the sounds of Arabic, harsh and melodic at the same time, as completely unintelligible to me as the crashing of ocean waves.

Unable to understand what is being said, full to the brim with rice and lamb and pine nuts, hummus and eggplant and baklava, still jet-lagged from our long journey to the Middle East, I find myself unbearably sleepy. My eyes close, yearning to stay that way; my head nods as I drift into unconsciousness.

Oh my God, I have to stay awake! I rub my eyes and give myself a series of small shakes to try to counteract the overwhelmingly soporific effect of the foreign language that surrounds me—murmurings like white noise only punctuated now and then by laughter and the clink of tiny silver teaspoons.

Finally, the kindly voice of our hostess inquires something of me in the Arabic I find incomprehensible. My husband has to translate: "Would you like to rest in the guest room?"

I attempt to resist their concern, to deny my sleepiness, but cannot. In the end, mortified, I'm forced to exchange the animation of the salon for the hushed isolation of an empty bedroom.

Fear of Military Presence

Returning one afternoon from a country estate an hour from the city center, we're stopped at a checkpoint by soldiers wearing khaki uniforms and bearing automatic rifles. Our host, a twentysomething cousin, pulls the car over and opens his window. From the back, where I sit with my husband, I try to figure out what's happening.

The cousin argues with the military guard. Their tones escalate. The cousin, our host, the person responsible for delivering us safely back to our hotel, is getting angry, seemingly outraged by the way the soldier is treating him in front of guests.

"What's going on?" I ask my husband in a near whisper, my voice taut with anxiety. He ignores me, stroking his upper lip with his index finger, a habit I know he unconsciously indulges in when stressed.

The placating voice of the cousin's wife in the front passenger seat seems to plead with her defiant husband to calm down and take it easy. He ignores her. A second soldier joins the first and barks at our host. I watch as he reluctantly steps out of the car.

"What the *hell* is happening?" I demand, this time much more forcefully, my anxiety having ratcheted up. Again, I'm ignored. I continue to watch, seething with anger and frustration, as well as racked with worry and fear, while men with machine guns force our charming host into the dark interior of a tent set up by the side of the highway. The host's wife and my husband confer over the car seat in rapid Arabic.

Furious now, I jab my husband with my elbow until he tells me that he's not sure what's going on and will translate later, when things quiet down.

Finally, the young man returns. As he enters the car, the soldiers who have accompanied him back seem to give him a parting warning. Ignoring them, he slams the door shut and turns the key in the ignition.

All is quiet as we shoot down the endless concrete strip bordered by farmed fields, olive tree groves, and distant brown hills. I wait in silence for my husband to talk to me, to explain what happened and why, to assuage my anxiety with translation and facts. But he never does.

Fear of Breaking Down

Later that night, dressed for dinner and sitting at an elegant table in the Sheraton courtyard, listening to my in-laws converse with close friends who have joined us at the outdoor restaurant with its stone fountain and bright bougainvillea, I struggle to hold it together.

Earlier, back in our hotel room, my husband and I argued. All my frustration at my inability to understand Arabic, to know what was being said and discussed by those around me, rose to the surface and found an outlet in blaming my husband. He, however, seemed unable to understand my position, unable to empathize with the stress and anxiety of *not knowing*. We had finished our fight unresolved, both left with the unease of mutual misunderstanding.

Now, at the restaurant, once again surrounded by this language that for me acts as a wall rather than a door, a barrier rather than a bridge, I blink rapidly and bite my cheek, pinching my wrist under a napkin to keep from breaking down.

Finally I can pretend no longer, and I flee the table.

In the restaurant's sleek marbled bathroom, I cry and cry, leaning against the sink, periodically plucking fresh tissues from a handy container and throwing the wet crumpled ones into the bin, until I begin to worry about myself, *When will I stop?* Tears keep flowing and I'm obliged to blow my nose over and over as I recall sitting in the hot car at the checkpoint, trying to decipher what was happening by reading the body language, the changing facial expressions, the shifting tones of voice of the various actors in the tense drama unfolding before me. The guns, the military tent, the uniforms, the tightly laced combat boots—all these had triggered my imagination and I had envisioned, in a kind of quiet panic, violence and humiliation, bruises and blood, arrest and disappearance. I had remembered hearing the rumors: *You know, Syrian prisons are supposed to be even worse than Israeli ones.*

My face still damp and my mascara smudged, I am attempting to make myself presentable enough to return to the table when the mother of the family dining with us enters the bathroom. She is classy, inside and out. She wears a hijab, covering her hair with an elegant European-style turban, her thin, kind face made up discreetly.

This family friend, until this evening a stranger to me, does not ask me to explain, or to say what's wrong, but comforts me instead with her presence and her small talk, deliberately distracting me as she helps pat my face dry with yet another tissue before hugging me close in a tight embrace.

Fear of Failure

Back home, it occurs to me that my in-laws have tested me—not deliberately, but as surely as if they'd handed me a blue book and asked me to write a five-paragraph essay on their homeland, so different from mainstream America with its orderly airports and enforced driving laws, endless efficient highways and towering skyscrapers, no-smoking areas and recycling campaigns. I realize that I've passed this test by taking certain aspects of Damascene culture—the dusty heat and the late nights, the women in trench coats and headscarves, the autocratic dictator and the censoring of one's conversation, the lack of seat belts in taxis and the lack of toilet paper in non-Western restrooms—in stride. Yet I know, in my heart, that *they* are the ones who have failed a test. By failing to adequately prepare me, despite my many queries before we left the States, for what I would encounter after clearing customs.

By failing to recognize my need for assurance. By failing to respect my need to know. By failing to translate. They have failed a test I didn't even know that they would be taking or that I would be judging.

Fear of the Future

I couldn't know it then, but I should have feared the future. I should have feared the ransacking of Iraq by the United States and the rise of ISIS, Syria's failed Arab Spring and Assad Jr.'s brutal repression of his own people. I should have feared the over five hundred thousand dead and the thirteen million fled. I should have feared the largest refugee population in human history. I should have feared the bombing of Palmyra—the stunning golden-red remains of a major cultural center of the ancient world—where my husband and I took photos of magnificent ruins, worthy of Olympia, among endless sand dunes. I should have feared the emptied streets where once I strolled in the balmy evenings scented with jasmine, happily licking my pistachio *booza*, the Syrian ice cream made elastic and sticky with milk, salep, mastic, and sugar. I should have feared the abandoned apartments once inhabited by loving and prosperous families, where I had visited, sitting under ornate crystal chandeliers at tables covered with intricately embroidered cloth and laden with plate upon plate of hummus and kibbeh, *ful* and *fattoush*, *maqluba* and *mahalabia*. I should have feared not being able to take to Damascus my own children, my sons who are half Syrian, to experience for themselves the vibrant hub of their father's heritage and their own birthright, the legacy of generations extending back over centuries.

How to Hang an Ayah

READER, I MARRIED A MUSLIM. Was that the day my innocence began to erode?

Sometime in 1990, two years before our wedding, my husband and his family drive from Atherton to Seattle for his residency interview. They fight about me in the car. There is shouting. In the hotel that night there is more fighting about me, and more shouting: mother and father against son. In his rage, the father pulls the phone from the wall and throws it across the room. I am too Western, too white, too Christian. I don't speak Arabic, I am not Muslim, I am not Syrian. They oppose me on principle: I will not make a good wife for their firstborn son.

At one time, my husband's father wanted to follow the outdated tradition of arranging a marriage between cousins. Her name was Laila. At another time, my husband was engaged to the daughter of a wealthy Lebanese family. Her name was Yasmine. But there were demands from Yasmine's father: one hundred thousand dollars a year to the young couple . . . a house . . . a full-time cleaner . . . an expensive car. My husband tired of the materialism and broke off the engagement.

Then there was me. My husband, worried about his parents' reaction, didn't introduce me to them for the first four years of our relationship.

Now, older and the mother of two sons myself, I can see the fear behind their outrage—fear for their son, for his happiness. What if I was too different? What if I was, like so many Western women in their eyes, individualistic and egocentric, putting self before family? What if I was cold and impersonal and aloof? What if I took their son away from them?

I sometimes think of innocence as a kind of layer of the self, or perhaps a type of aura, with which we are born. It's like our mother's womb is Paradise and we are all born a blank slate, free of the knowledge that we will acquire almost immediately as we emerge, naked and bloody and shrieking, into the world. When I was younger, I didn't realize what was happening as it happened; I didn't see that my innocence of the ways of the world—weaponized religions, parents feuding against children, stereotypes feeding exclusion—was eroding, slowly disappearing in the face of time and experience.

MY MOTHER BAPTIZED MY firstborn son when he was just an infant. It had always bothered her that I hadn't. When he was five months old, we took a family vacation to Italy. She was taking a turn carrying him as we toured the Vatican, stopping in the Sistine Chapel to gaze upward at Adam receiving the spark of life from his bearded Creator. The restoration of the frescoes was newly complete, and they glowed as if reborn, liberated after centuries from the dull, dark layers of dirt, dust, and time.

When I noticed my mother scurry down one of the hallways out of the chapel, I followed her to a niche where she stood half hidden in the shadows, my baby in her arms. She had found a font of holy water and was busily baptizing her grandchild before his Muslim father caught her. Dipping her fingers in the font, she wet his brow with the holy water while making the sign of the cross over his head: *Yo te bautizo en el nombre del Padre, del Hijo, y del Espíritu Santo, Amén.*

IN SEVENTH GRADE, MY CLASS watched a movie called *A Thief in the Night* about the Second Coming of the Messiah. My school was a missionary school in Quito, Ecuador, run by Evangelicals. All day we heard about God the Father and his son Jesus Christ; we prayed and read the Bible in religion class; we were encouraged to accept Jesus as our "Personal Savior" and be baptized. The movie depicted the "Rapture," the future moment when the faithful, the true Christians, will be spirited up to heaven, corporeal bodies and all, leaving behind those who don't believe. In a split second, families will be separated—wives from husbands, sisters from brothers, children from parents.

That evening, I asked my father if he believed in God. To my horror, he said no. He told me he was an "atheist"—someone who believes that there is no God, and that nothing exists after death. Later, lying in my bed in the dark, I couldn't stop crying. It hurt too much to imagine my father left behind, or in hell. At one point my mother came into my room and sat on the edge of my bed. She comforted me as she always did, reassuring me with whatever it took, even half-truths or outright lies.

"Don't worry," she said. "When he is an old man he will return to the Church. Everyone returns to God when they are old."

IT'S 9/11. I'M ONE OF THOSE people who sits in front of the screen for hours at a time. As an adult, I don't cry easily, but on this day I cry so much that my eyes swell and my nose chaps from constant blowing. I'm shattered by the images on the news, and I'm also afraid for my son, who sits in front of me playing with his bulldozers and excavators. He is not yet two years old.

"Why did we give him a Muslim name?" I wail at my husband when he comes home from work. "Why not Oscar or Harry?"

A few weeks later, I see a young man in a white pickup truck. On its sides he has used blue duct tape to write in huge letters that run from hood to trunk: NUKE THEM ALL.

Almost a year afterward, I'm driving from our home in Medina to Seattle. We cross the bridge spanning Lake Washington and make the long turn toward the city. Finally the cityscape comes into view, silhouetted against the gray sky. From the back seat I hear my son say, "Those buildings are going to burn down." I thought he wasn't watching, that he wasn't interested, that he was distracted by his cars and dinosaurs, that he was too young in any case to be impacted by the television screen. I was wrong.

ISLAM IN THE UNITED STATES IS like a sapling bay in a vast forest of giant sequoias. Its culture can be overwhelmed, dominated by Judeo-Christian surroundings, made invisible. Because my husband feared that Islam in our family, for our children, would be engulfed, rendered anemic and dismissible by Christmas trees and decorations, presents and nutcrackers, even menorahs and dreidels, he refused to have a Christmas tree in our house.

To my relief, by the time my children were aware of Christmas and decorated trees, we lived two minutes by car and ten minutes by foot up the hill from my parents. With them we could celebrate December 25 with tree selection at the local lot (everyone chiming in with their opinions); tree decoration with hot chocolate and a fire specially lit in the fireplace; and Christmas mornings of opening presents, drinking cup after cup of tea, and listening to the classic carols from my father's collection playing on the stereo.

The only time we ever had a tree in our house was the winter after I completed chemo. When I mentioned how cozy it would be to have our own tree, my husband relented, probably because he felt sorry for me with my cropped hair and sparse eyebrows. My sons and I chose a small, shapely Douglas fir, which we took home and decorated with newly bought ornaments, all golds and ruby reds. The tree glowed at night, lit from within by a long string of tiny lights. Since then we've reverted to holiday merrymaking solely at my parents' house; my sons don't seem to notice, and I don't mind.

THE FIRST TIME I HEARD THE Muslim call to prayer, I was in Damascus. There is nothing quite like hearing it live from an imam calling out from a minaret high above the streets and souks of the city. It was breathtakingly beautiful and arresting. It seemed to command attention and reverence. Never mind that most people around me continued about their business unmoved. It remained a plea for a moment of mindfulness, of acknowledging the spirit, of communing with the divine. I loved it when it woke me at dawn in my hotel room or, muffled by the walls and curtains, became a part of my dreams. I loved it in the middle of the day when it soared out and over the busy city, reminding us of greater things than the material. I loved it best at twilight, when it became a part of that in-between time of day, the sky tinged violet, the scent of jasmine wafting stronger in the waning afternoon.

I heard it next in Alexandria and Cairo and Istanbul. It never ceased to make me pause and listen. Sometimes, if I could, I would close my eyes, the better to absorb the voice and the melody that seemed to hold so much—nostalgia, sadness, history, hope.

I heard it too in California, in the Atherton home of my husband's family. My father-in-law was dead. His body lay in the master bedroom on a hospital cot, naked except for a diaper that I chose to see as a sort of loincloth. The room was darkened by the drawn drapes, hushed by the thick carpet and the gloom. The widow and her sons spoke in whispers. The one consistent sound was the Quran as it played from the speakers on my mother-in-law's writing desk. My husband told me it had been playing all day, for hours before his father died. In his last moments he had been enveloped, as if in an embrace, by the musical recital of his faith.

Forty days after his death, the family held a memorial gathering at their home, as is the custom. My husband and children and I were there, naturally, as were my brother-in-law, his wife, and their daughters. There were friends from all stages of my parents-in-law's life.

It happened to be the month of Ramadan, so many of the guests were fasting. When the time came to break the fast, one of the family's closest friends, a mother of three grown Syrian American children, approached my ten-year-old son with a plate of dates. "Here," she said in her Arabic accent, "take this and pass it around to the grown-ups."

My son, after glancing at me, walked around the room, balancing the plate of dates carefully in both hands. It is the practice to eat a date at the start of breaking one's fast. I hadn't known this; my son hadn't known this.

Later that night, my brother-in-law and his wife complained about this same woman chastising their daughter when she misbehaved. I could not join in their indignation at her bossiness—I was delighted that someone maternal and Arab and Muslim had cared enough to teach my son how to navigate an unfamiliar cultural moment.

I AM WATCHING WHEN MY son is confronted, for the first time, by a life-size statue of Christ on the Cross. He is eleven years old. Standing in front of it, he looks for a while, taking in the bloody wounds, the thorny crown, the nailed feet. After a bit, he returns to where I'm sitting and asks me, "Who is that man?"

At that moment, I realize that my husband and I have succeeded in bringing up our children completely without religion, in a secular void. It's a dizzying concept, as I only truly know my own upbringing—one saturated with religion, with my mother and grandmother's Catholicism as well as the missionary fervor of my middle school's Evangelicalism. I can't remember a time when I did not know about the Crucified Christ, Mary the Mother of God, or the Holy Trinity.

I tell my son what I can think of on the spot—that Jesus was a great leader who believed in kind and radical equality, and as such he became a threat and was killed by those frightened by the power of his message.

I'VE ONLY GONE TO CONFESSION ONCE, as part of my First Communion. Did I and the rest of the children confess beforehand, so that we could receive the Body of Christ in a pure state? I know I was dressed all in white—white veil and dress, white patent leather shoes, white ankle socks—the color that in our culture signifies purity.

Long before that day, of course, my mother made sure I was baptized into the Catholic Church. The single photo memorializing the event shows my mother, who is holding me in her arms, with my grandmother and the priest.

Looking back, it's a blessing that I was only made to confess once; it felt awkward and made me uncomfortable to enter the dark, close space, kneel at the miniature pew, and listen for the guidance I had been told would come. When it did come, it emanated from a disembodied voice, strange and male. Fortunately, we were given precise instructions in our catechism classes and I knew to recite, like a parrot, the "sins" I had committed before asking to be forgiven.

I CAN NEVER UNDERSTAND THE WAY my parents-in-law opposed their son's marriage to me when I think about their past. My mother-in-law came from a wealthy family; at one point, her grandfather's Damascene household included concubines and Christian slaves. My father-in-law had to work for money starting at a young age. She was Sunni and he was Shi'a. She had rich suitors whom she categorically refused, despite their lavish gifts and extravagant promises. He fell in love with her intellect and her beauty at their university. She was attracted by his revolutionary ideals. He soon had a price on his head for his subversive activism. Her brother was the chief of police, and for the love of his sister he helped the couple escape to Egypt. They eloped by driving her Volkswagen Beetle to the base of the mountains and traveling the rest of the way on foot. They were, for that time in Syria, yin and yang, oil and water, black and white. They came from different classes, conflicting versions of Islam, and warring political factions. How, then, could they oppose my marrying their son?

MY CHILDREN AND I ACCOMPANY my husband on a work trip to Alexandria. There, my husband's Egyptian colleague takes us to the Sporting Club, a huge park in the middle of the city that reminds me a little of New York's Central Park, except that it's more contained and offers a mosque, two restaurants, a polo field, an Olympic pool, and several playgrounds for the children.

It's a Friday, the only day off for Egyptians. There is a sandstorm somewhere near Cairo, and we feel it in the white, misty air; sometimes my teeth crunch unexpectedly on a grain of sand.

Around midday, we hear the call to prayer. Our host, a jolly father of two, asks if my husband and older son would like to pray with them in the nearby mosque. My husband hesitates, discomfited, but I encourage him to go, and to take our son. I want him to experience some of his Middle Eastern heritage by praying with his father in a mosque.

Yet as they leave and I watch their backs recede, I worry about him. I hope that his father will guide him through the motions of Muslim prayer: the positioning, the kneeling, the genuflecting. That he won't feel awkward or strange or alone.

WHAT MY PARENTS-IN-LAW DIDN'T realize before I married their son, when there was so much strife around the idea of his marrying me, was that we are actually quite compatible. We both are familiar with non-white, non-American belief systems and ways of living. Growing up, I identified primarily with my Peruvian mother over my Anglo father and listened, enthralled, as she recounted stories about her childhood in Arequipa and Lima, a childhood that included gallops on Moro the horse at the hacienda, constant piano practice, nuns in a boarding school, and summer days on the beach eating *anticuchos* and *picarones*.

We are both attached to our families. I cried for two hours straight the first day of our honeymoon because I missed my mother. I dreamt about my family in California every night for a week when I first moved to Seattle. My husband saw me only on Saturdays for years when we were dating because he felt bad about leaving his parents alone on weekends. He still calls his mother every day, no matter what, wherever he is.

In terms of religion, we are both lapsed. I don't practice Catholicism; he doesn't practice Islam. We have been shaped by the cultures of our religions, certainly, but we don't actively live their rituals and regulations. We both are academics, and we constantly discuss culture, politics, history.

We love tea and drink it all day long. On weekends we insist on teatime, when we sit for a bit in the middle of the morning with cups of Assam or English breakfast and talk, our whole family, or if our sons are not around, just him and me.

OUR HOUSE REPRESENTS US as a couple. You only have to look at our décor, the furniture and the art, to know us. Persian rugs and Peruvian mirrors complement each other perfectly; carved bronze vases from Syria set off hammered silver trays from Peru. There is a harmony, I like to think, in our house that reflects a harmony in our union.

I have a young friend in her twenties who is like a daughter to me. Perhaps because she is a child of divorce, this daughter-friend loves to comment on the interior of my house; to reflect on the way our collection of furniture represents us and our marriage; to discuss, once again, how the side table inlaid with mother-of-pearl from Damascus and the carved leather coffee table from Lima together enhance the look of our living room. It gives her a satisfaction I share, that of an intertwining of two parts to make a greater whole.

WE DO HAVE A QURAN IN OUR house, as well as a Bible. They are more decorative than instructive. We also have a plaque carved with the words of an *ayah*. An ayah is a verse from the Quran, and ours is the most famous one, about God's infinite love for us all. When it came time to find a place for it in our house, my husband, knowing exactly where to put it, took the carved wooden plaque with the beautiful Arabic script his mother gave us and hung it carefully above the doorframe of the front entrance to our house.

Exile

My father-in-law wears olive-green slacks with his houndstooth jacket over a cashmere sweater. He's all dressed up with nowhere to go. I take that back—that's not really true. He does have somewhere to go. But it's a poor substitute for where he would be going if he hadn't emigrated from Syria, if he had never left Damascus. It's a poor substitute for where he wants to be going. Some would say it's a poor substitute for where he should be going.

I never knew the Damascus of my father-in-law, or, for that matter, of my mother-in-law. The closest I came to knowing that Damascus was through visiting the city of their childhood in the early years of my marriage to their son. Back then, in the 1990s, the death and destruction that occurred after the Syrian attempt to join the Arab Spring had not yet happened. That Damascus was a Damascus that still retained its old-world flavor of close-knit families and crowded, labyrinthine souks, of ripe oranges squeezed into a glass while you waited outside the market. It was a Damascus of long, leisurely lunches late in the afternoon, with family and often friends gathered at heavily laden tables to share the hummus and the lamb, as well as community gossip and the news of the day. It was a Damascus of evening strolls smelling jasmine and licking ice cream cones, of sitting at outdoor cafés drinking sweet black *shai* from delicate glass teacups while stray cats dozed under the tables.

Of course I understood even then that my father-in-law's Damascus was much more than what I could absorb in the two short weeks I was there. I know from his stories that his was a Damascus where he got a job as a young teenager because his family was poor. His was a Damascus where, oppressed by the dominant party's politics, he joined a revolutionary group to try to effect change. His was a Damascus where he only met his future wife on campus because her older brother had fought for her to be there, demanding that their father allow his little sister to attend university. His was a Damascus where he eventually earned a price on his head for subversive activities and learned to fear for his life. In his Damascus, my father-in-law was able to marry his beloved, despite her father's vehement protestations against his class and his Shiite beliefs, only because she was willing to elope with him over mountains and across borders so that he would be safe.

THERE'S A STARBUCKS AT THE Stanford Shopping Center. Already, in the early 2000s, people sit at their individual tables, walled off by earbuds and laptops, with faces glued to screens and minds focused elsewhere. I feel sorry for my father-in-law going to this café that is so like thousands of others around the world, bland, homogenous, baldly capitalist. I feel sad for him as he enters eagerly, this being part of his routine, his self-imposed schedule, that is supposed to be fun and entertaining, a break from errands and domesticity and the isolation of his own home. I feel bad for him entering this café with such high expectations, albeit by this time ones already quashed by experience.

For no one looks up at him with welcome or recognition. No one looks up at all. No one smiles upon seeing him walk through the swinging glass door or calls out his name. He walks unacknowledged to the counter to order coffee from an indifferent employee. Eventually he will take his steaming cup to a table, where he will sit alone. He has brought a book with him in anticipation of the silence and boredom that awaits him. But before opening it to the page he'd dog-eared the day prior, he looks around him as he shakes two packets of sugar into his coffee and mixes it with a tiny plastic straw. He searches for another person who is sitting alone, perhaps similarly bored and lonely. If he finds an open face, he will try to start a conversation, maybe about the weather or the quality of the coffee or last night's news. He is looking for communication, for connection, wanting to replicate what he would have if he were back in Damascus.

Right before he leaves the house, my father-in-law sits on the carved Syrian chair by the huge front door. He puts on his shoes with some effort, bending awkwardly over his hefty paunch and relying on a shoehorn to complete the task. After he stands, which he accomplishes by leaning with a grunt on the console next to him, he grabs his keys and announces his departure. "I am going now. I will be at the shopping center. Meet me there later. Bring your mother-in-law." He says this in a thick accent, almost every word of his second language still proving unwieldy after decades in England and the United States.

I happen to witness both his shoe-donning ritual and his parting speech from upstairs, where there is a large bridgeway that overlooks the entrance. He knows I'm there because he can hear my toddler playing with the wooden train set.

I lean over the railing. "Okay! Have a good day!" I am cheery but avoid committing to meeting him at the coffee shop. I don't know how my day will play out. In any case, he will call his wife several times in the next hour with his flip phone until she agrees to join him.

He grunts a goodbye, not impressed with me—his Catholic, half-white, English-speaking daughter-in-law—as the sole witness to his departure, much preferring anyone else in his immediate family (one of his sons, definitely, or his wife) to me.

If my father-in-law were living in Damascus he would also be going to a café, maybe at the centuries-old souk, maybe at a modern mall, maybe even to one that is part of a Starbucks-like chain. But the difference is that he would be meeting his friends. Probably childhood friends or close colleagues. Maybe also his relatives—brothers and brothers-in-law, cousins, younger uncles, and older nephews. Family who are also friends and friends who are like family. Who have lived what he has lived. Who worship the way he worships. Who eat the same foods cooked in the same ways. Who speak the same language.

As he entered that café, the one in Damascus, his friends would look up and smile, calling out to him, *Ahlan wa Sahlan!* and pull up a chair for him at their table. Together, they would sit for hours smoking cigarettes and drinking Turkish coffee, talking politics while patting their old-man bellies.

THE EXILE DREAMS OF DEATH. He dreams of death in his homeland. This happens after all chance of returning to live permanently in the mother country has ended. There are left only sporadic visits and possible retirement. The exile gets too old to hope for a full life back in his country. And he has children. These children grow up and learn and assimilate in the new country, the host country, the foreign, alien country. What does this make them? Also alien? Also foreign? This is part of the immigrant's pain. His children can be different from him—linguistically, culturally, and psychologically—yet these very children are the ties that bind him inexorably to the new country, the alien culture. How does the exile choose between the metaphorical mother, which is country, culture, and language, and the physical child, who has come to mean family, devotion, and love?

My father-in-law wanted to end his life in Syria, or at least in nearby Lebanon. But never in the United States, never in the West. He wanted to die in the Middle East, in the heart of the Arabic language, his mother tongue, and Islam, his one true faith. Instead he now lies buried in a desolate spot off Interstate 580 in Livermore, one of the only two Muslim graveyards in the Bay Area.

It's an ugly place. Hot and windy. There are no trees, there is no shade, there is nowhere to sit. Only bald plots, some covered in fake grass, others decorated with dusty tubs of plastic flowers.

I OPEN THE FRONT DOOR TO WELCOME the worker who has come to install our bedroom shades. He introduces himself—"Hello, my name is Wasseem"—then steps inside, automatically taking off his shoes at the entrance. His English is excellent, his accent soft. His voice instantly makes me feel nostalgic for the Middle East I've come to know from stories and visits.

For a moment I'm back in Alexandria with my family at the Syrian bakery we've discovered, leaning over gleaming glass shelves of Arabic desserts, *baqlawa* and *kanafeh* and *maamool*. Leaving with our plastic bags full of glistening pastries. Ambling past the café whose courtyard is filled with palms and potted plants, where trendy twentysomethings are gathered in the growing darkness around small tables, talking and laughing under the lantern lights, the smoke from the hookahs curling around their heads. Joining the groups of Egyptians, friends and lovers and families, on the Corniche just as the first notes of the call to prayer emanate from the many minarets scattered across the city.

My mind recalls all this, and I'm feeling the pull of this far-away culture, even as I ask the young man before me if he's from the Middle East.

"Yes," he says, "I come from Lebanon!"

I'm conscious of the Quranic verse engraved on a plaque that my husband has placed over the entryway. I wonder if he is Muslim but don't ask, my curiosity having some respect left for personal boundaries. Later I will look up his name, Wasseem, and find out that it is a Muslim name meaning graceful and handsome and lucky.

When Wasseem is finished with the shades, I walk with him back to the driveway where his truck is parked. We linger for a moment at the bottom of the stairs, and our chitchat segues to his home in Lebanon.

"I miss Bayrūt very much!" he says.

I look at him. By this time he is sitting on the stairs, his head in his hands. "I know," I say. "This culture is cold . . . everyone is isolated." I turn my gaze to a nearby window, envisioning an "America" out there that is all work and stress and living paycheck to paycheck, without family, without community. When do we have time to stroll a boardwalk on a weeknight? When do we see family and friends for hours at a time? When do we put our jobs and our worries aside to relax and just be?

"But what can I do?" he says. "I cannot go back."

I ponder this. "Do you have children?"

He tells me he has one boy who is five years old.

"Then it's not too late!" I say. "You can still go back, your son won't know the difference—he won't blame you for taking him away from his school or his friends."

Wasseem shakes his head. “What is there to go back to? What is there for me in Bayrūt?”

I think about the recent explosion that rocked the city like an earthquake. I think about the worldwide pandemic, about the assassinations of politicians, about the bombs, about the rotting garbage piling up on sidewalks for months, about the civil war whose effects are still felt.

I have no answer for him.

First Times

I WAS ELEVEN YEARS OLD the first time I saw hell.

My father liked taking the family on weekend excursions that often involved a cultural experience. Thus I found myself in a Catholic church in the historical part of Quito. At the time—forty years ago, when my family lived in Ecuador—this historical section had not yet been restored and was, especially to my immature eyes, grimy and dirty. All I noticed as we walked to the church were the scraps of newspaper blowing about, the smells of urine, the skeletal dogs, mangy cats, and broken glass. Beggars reached out, invoking God's blessing. Some of the children, of vendors or beggars, many with bare feet and torn clothing, paused in their play to stare.

I was relieved to enter the church, to pass through the heavy wooden doors and into the soft, perpetual twilight inside. Voices, even footsteps, were subdued there; solemn saints from centuries past gazed at the visitors from paintings, as statues, through stained glass, and down from the frescoed ceiling.

As I turned toward a deserted corner of the hushed church, peaceful after the noise and sun of the city streets outside, I saw it. A painting. Huge and bleak and gruesome. Demons tormented human souls with vicious excitement. Anguish was made tangible through fire and bondage—spears and shackles and chains and pits. Victims were objects—broken, thrown, torn, crushed.

Suffocating, I turned back to the center of the church with its more familiar paintings of martyred saints, Madonnas and their bleeding hearts, and Christs with crowns of thorns for relief, but failed to find any. I was forced to go back through the doors and return to what had become, in a few short minutes, a comforting and ordinary scene outside.

THIRTY-TWO YEARS LATER, MY older son is eleven. I've brought my family to South America to visit my relatives and to introduce them to my Ecuadorian past and Peruvian heritage. We're scheduled to view the catacombs at the Convento de San Francisco in Lima today. I'm worried. I don't want my children to be traumatized. I feel the familiar clenching in my stomach from conflicting concerns: Is it a mistake to tour the catacombs, like a family would a Disneyland ride, with an eight- and an eleven-year-old? Will it be too much for my sons, still so young, to descend into the underground crypts and walk through grisly piles of human bones—tibias and ulnas and femurs and skulls—arranged by type? Will they realize that these buried bones represent entire lives and whole personalities, once alive, now dead? Or will this tour be educational? An exposure to the history of Peru and the culture of Catholicism?

We go anyway; it seems, as usual, that I am the only adult in the group obsessed with these worries. I determine to keep an eye on the children, to see if I need to swoop in at any point to soothe anxieties with softening fairy-tale explanations for the mounds of human bones.

We arrive at the entrance to the monastery, where we purchase tickets for the catacombs tour and wait for our guide. As we sit, side by side, on the hard wooden benches lining the vestibule's wall, my older son gets up and approaches a life-size statue of the Crucified Christ across the room. I watch him with curiosity. What is he thinking? He passes back and forth in front of the statue a couple of times, observing, analyzing. I watch him as he takes in the drooping head, the thorny crown, the blood dripping down the face, the side, the palms and feet. I see him consider the naked torso, the thin arms and legs, the protruding ribs and concave belly. What does he make of the pierced forehead? The wounded side? The nails and the cross?

Because my husband and I are both lapsed in our respective religions, we decided before we married to bring up our children without any religious training. I have never taken my sons to church, Catholic or Protestant; I have never told them about Christ, Martyr or Savior; I've never read to them from the Bible, Old Testament or New; I've never shown them religious images, of Jesus or Joseph, Mary or Moses. And now, in this moment I see the Christ on the Cross, an image so familiar that I take it for granted, as if for the first time. I'm startled to realize that this figure that is so well-known and has often been comforting to me is actually frightful, repulsive.

My son returns, his face questioning, to ask, "Who is that man? Why is he hanging there?"

How to respond? What to say? There is so much history, so much context, so much personal experience bound up in any answer to my son's question. I realize he has no language for what he is seeing. Unlike his mother, who can't remember *not* being intimate with the graphic details of Christ's execution, my son sees only the literal physicality of the statue in front of him.

I decide to go the sociopolitical route. "His name is Jesus," I say, hoping for a calm, casual tone, "and he was a great man who had a vision to make the world better for everyone. He lived hundreds of years ago, and his philosophy about love was so different that it threatened the people in power. And when people are threatened, they get scared. So they killed him."

My son ponders my words for a few moments and then, apparently satisfied, or perhaps merely bored, leaves me to go poke at his little brother.

After we've finished touring the catacombs and looking at the arrangements of bleached bones preserved in the chilled, dank air, the boys think only of getting ice cream and going home. I stop an ice cream vendor bicycling his cart through the streets, and they make their selections carefully.

I hear them, as they bite into their Popsicles with satisfaction, talk about the "catacoombas." They soon segue into composing a little ditty, whose lyrics consist solely of the word "catacoombas" repeated indefinitely—"Cata*coom*bas! Cata*coom*bas!" they sing.

So much for a traumatic experience, I think to myself.

A WEEK PASSES AND WE'RE IN downtown Quito, poised to visit the very same church that houses the painting that for years occupied my nightmares, and even some of my conscious fears. I insist that the boys stay outside on the steps of the church with their father while I enter first, on a sort of reconnaissance mission, to see if the painting is still there. I find myself holding my breath as I cross the same threshold and turn toward the same corner from decades ago.

And there it is. Still hanging in the same place on the same wall, still depicting the same hellish landscape of a Catholic artist's imagination. But I am surprised to see that it is . . . small. So much smaller than the one, massive and overpowering, of my memories. Have I grown or has it shrunk? I feel like Alice after falling down the rabbit hole—disoriented. Nevertheless, calling my children into the church, I make sure to position myself between them and the painting, guiding them past the dark corner toward the light of the nave beyond.

The Flinch

ALTHOUGH IT WAS COLD, and I was outside, the heat rose up through me, that hot surge of shame that ends with a flush in the cheeks.

A new friend had just asked about the charm I wear on my wrist.

This charm is a tooth. A baby tooth. White and smooth, it hangs from a link on my bracelet. I'd never before thought to question the Peruvian tradition of wearing that particular type of charm; until then I had understood it only as a representation of the maternal bond, of the love between mother and child. Flesh of my flesh, bone of my bone, a charm to claim my children as always mine, small and tender-looking—pretty, like a pearl or a bit of shimmery shell. Set in 22-karat gold, a tiny talisman claiming a stake in the maternal self.

But that easy embrace of a familial and cultural tradition changed when my new friend asked about the charm hanging from my wrist and then . . . flinched.

We were sitting, my new friend and I, outside my recently purchased home, on a terraced portion of the hillside garden. It was a fall day, in the afternoon, and the air was chilly. But the children wanted to play, and the interior of the house was only sparsely decorated, as we had no money at the time to invest in a designer, whole sets of matching furniture, or even a nice sofa. The bedrooms had only mattresses on the floor and our living room was empty save for a brass urn I'd bought years earlier from under the noses of a stylish couple at a Neiman Marcus sale. (Later, my Syrian father-in-law would praise my eye in recognizing this quality piece and I would carry his approbation inside me, like a glowing coal, for years.)

The terraced bit of garden on which my new friend and I sat was supposed to be a patio, but was only a poor imitation of one at that time, having been molded, literally, from the claylike soil and pounded into a semblance of a flat deck. There was no railing or flagstone, just a drop from the edge of pressed dirt. From this vantage point we could see as far as the skinny white Campanile, UC Berkeley's signature tower, across the bay. I had placed on the dirt a couple of teak patio chairs brought from our small backyard in Seattle, and the two of us sitting on them resembled a pair of birds perched on a cliff, the wind chilling our skin and goosebumping our flesh, our noses threatening to run and our eyes to water as we strove to chat companionably about our children, their teachers, the school.

Then came the moment when this new friend noticed my charm. This was a charm that my mother had three of herself, one for each of her own children. A charm that my mother and I had planned even before my sons were born. One for which I had given her my toddler's baby tooth to have set in gold in Peru, where it was a common type of adornment. A charm that she had brought back, packed with loving care, in a small velvet jewelry bag.

It is fascinating and strange to me how a mere gesture, a small movement, an oh-so-slight recoil can cause, like a finger in a socket, that surge charged with shame. The actual moment was subtle, barely discernible, even though it felt to me like a slap in the face. The person who flinched, this school-parent friend, would never have been obvious in her distaste. She was too polite. Too reserved to exhibit judgment beyond the slightest widening of the eyes, a tiny lift of the eyebrows, the centimeter of movement back—at most the suggestion of a gesture rather than a crude, obvious sign. In Spanish, the word used for disrespectful or rude is *malcriada,* which literally translates into badly brought up or badly raised. My Anglo American friend had been, within her family's traditions, *bién criada*.

THE FIRST TIME I SAW MEREDITH as an adult was during a tour of a garden carefully cultivated to be viewed and appreciated, even coveted. This garden tour was part of an annual fundraiser for the aforementioned school, the school where one of my sons and one of hers shared a grade. In some ways Meredith had grown up to be my doppelgänger. Same age. Tall like me. Dark hair and eyes. Serious, if not quite bookish. Native of the same small town. Graduate of the same large university. For a few years, decades prior, we'd even shared an elementary class in the same school our boys now attended. Yet there were key differences.

Meredith had short hair. Straight and shiny and neatly trimmed. *Contained*. Her whole persona was contained and controlled in a neat, WASP-y package. A couple of years later, when I knew her better, I asked her if she had always had short hair, if she was what I call a "short-hair person." She paused for a minute, as though she'd never been asked such a question before, then nodded. "I think I am. I can't imagine myself with long hair. It's always been short like this."

I asked her because I myself was a "long-hair person." My hair had always been a part of my sense of self and, thick and unruly, it was the polar opposite of Meredith's neat short cut, of her tidy poised persona.

That first day we met on the garden tour, after all those decades, she had on a white button-down shirt, crisp and clean, and a pair of pale khaki maternity slacks, for she was a few months pregnant with her fourth child. Diamond studs (requisite for our generation of affluent mothers) shone from her small, exposed ears, and the diamonds were stunning—large, but not too large, sparkling and clear—I would guess Cartier or Van Cleef & Arpels.

I wanted to continue the custom in my mother's family of setting children's baby teeth in gold and keeping them as a kind of amulet by wearing them as charms. What was so awful about this small, defenseless object? So offensive? What made it something to draw away from, to flinch at when first recognized for what it was? It may have been the perceived crudeness, the primitiveness of wearing a physical part of another person—a piece of bone, made from calcium, first grown in a mother's womb and then in a baby's mouth—as jewelry. Perhaps it was an association with superstitious practices that deemed the wearing of such a charm un-Christian, uncivilized. Or an association with the body and therefore the dirty, grotesque, or even sinful.

There exist various scenarios in my mind, but they are all assumptions. I can't really know, since I didn't ask. I would never have asked. It would have been too embarrassing—bringing my insecurity into the light, exposing my self-doubt. I also noted the Christian cross my friend wore that day, and realized how bizarre and pagan my tooth charm might seem in comparison.

Yet I had the urge to defend myself, even if only to myself, in the face of that judgment. If I had been in court, both as defendant and lawyer, I would have pointed out the underlying history of the Christian cross hanging from my friend's neck. I would have reminded the jury that the cross is a bloody symbol that has been sanitized not only by time and exposure and acculturation but also, in this case, by the platinum and diamonds from which it had been crafted, by the thin, elegant chain from which it hung as it rested on the smooth, perfumed skin of this white woman, this wealthy wife and mother, this critical tourist of cultivated gardens and automatic condemner of another's talismanic charm. Was it fair, I would have demanded the court, that I was to be judged for my innocent little piece of baby bone, one given up by my child's body willingly, appropriately, and naturally as superfluous, when my friend could wear—with approval and even admiration—a symbol originating in violence and gore?

If people are shaped by experience, by the way they are nurtured as well as by their genetic makeup, then I have been shaped by layers of indirect, implied shame, a sense of humiliation that arrives obliquely and stays backstage in the shadows, never venturing into direct sunlight so that it can be seen, recognized, and named. This is the way shame thrives—like a dank mushroom, a slippery, nocturnal creature, one that can exist only in the darkness and the shade.

The twisted layers of complicated shame in my life originate on my mother's side. Shame is a ball we have passed back and forth all my life, from mother to daughter, again and again. There are times I've rejected it, when I've tried to hit it out of the park, a home run, never to come back—but then, becoming a boomerang, it inevitably does.

My mother, born and raised in an elite class of Peruvians, educated by nuns, served by maids, taught English and horseback riding and piano, in this country strains toward whiteness, threatened always by the negative stereotypes that exist here in words like *immigrant* and *Hispanic* and *South American*. She lives a precarious balance, in between the past and the present, brown and white, Lima and

California, Spanish and English. She balances there always, as if on a tightrope between skyscrapers or a slippery ledge on a rocky mountainside. A woman in exile, having left her beloved Peru in her twenties to marry my father, she must constantly negotiate the racism here in Northern California, where brown people from Central and South America are stuck, for the most part, in the service sector. They maintain the gardens and clean the houses, they wipe the tables in restaurants and fix the engines of SUVs and sedans, but they never live in our kind of town, in our kind of house, with our kind of privilege.

My mother has her own prejudices, of course: She forbade me once I became a teenager from even setting foot on Haight Street, for example, fearing not only drugs and promiscuity but also grime and hippies. She'd flinch at things and people and ideas in the United States only to feel like an outsider, someone who didn't belong, who didn't understand, when others—the women in our town, the mothers of my classmates, those who spoke flawless English with only American accents—would flinch, literally or figuratively, at something about her.

Yet I myself own the flinch. It seems I have inherited it, an early bequest, from my mother. When I visit Lima as an adult, when I spend time with my mother's family and in my Peruvian relatives' homes, I often draw back, internally, with distaste at the things I hear and see: My aunt looking through her maids' bags before they leave for their homes, suspecting them of stealing. My cousin driving off in irritation when the light turns green after yelling out the window—*¡Demasiado tarde!*—at the ragged brown girl frantically searching through her boxes for the exact flavor of chewing gum my cousin had insisted on. Another cousin's friends, when all of us are sitting outside with drinks together one summer evening, talking about the "dirty Arabs," not knowing or not caring that I am married to one.

In the United States, I have flinched as well: In the morgue where my father-in-law lay when I saw a room full of urns for pet ashes next to the room full of urns for people's remains. At an acquaintance who threatened the principal of the elementary school with withholding much-needed donations if she wouldn't add Chinese to the curriculum. At a white friend of a white friend who, well-intentioned yet ignorant, still uses the word "mulatto."

I have periods of time when I believe myself free not only from my mother's prejudices—ones that she turns on people of different races or classes or nationalities with different customs and behaviors from her own—but also from the shame that is the other side of the coin. Clearly, however, as my friend's flinch showed me, I am not. This shame is the shame of the colonized and therefore the shame of imposed inferiority. It is the shame fed by fear: fear of exclusion, of embarrassment, of the faux pas. The back-and-forth movement between cultures, the constant negotiation of traditions and mores demanded of the immigrant, render weak and assailable my mother's standards of behavior and attire. I inherited these standards that could be questioned and judged, that could be deemed primitive or, even worse, tacky. It is in this space that the immigrant and her children live, the space between a sure, strong, established knowledge of the self, of the rightness of how one presents the self through dress or rituals or speech, and the feeling that one's culture, ways of being, and taste are wrong, aberrant, vulgar. I remain divided into two selves: the cerebral and the visceral. I know in my head what my values are—they are a blend of the maternal, the immigrant, the Peruvian, and also the paternal, the first world, the Anglo American. My mind feels no shame at the flinch; it is the body that reacts instinctively, the emotional self that has been trained since birth to look out for judgment and contempt.

So there I was, holding within myself the constant conflict between familial history and my mother's advice on the one hand and my own observations and experiences on the other, sitting on a chilly terrace on a wooden folding chair, making small talk with a woman who embodied, to my eyes, the successful wife-mother-WASP-yuppie.

Meredith was the daughter of one of those women whom my mother would avoid after moving to the town where we still live—the mothers of the other children at our local school, the mothers who knew what to say, what to do, and what to wear. My mother avoided these women, never making a single friend in our town or from our school, because she dreaded ostracization, gaze aversion, flinching. Like these women, Meredith seemed self-sufficient in her own person, *en su persona*; she seemed complacent in her own identity and looked satisfied, more than satisfied, with her own family, their spacious home, their big golden dog. Her living room had a grand piano in one corner, windows traditionally curtained with heavy drapes and valances, a large, finely worked carpet in dignified shades of blue and cream. Family photos in Tiffany frames adorned the Ethan Allen side tables artfully placed around the room. And this person—someone versed in thoroughbred culture, someone harking back to the American version of blue-blood heritage—saw the charm I wore and flinched.

It was so small that the entire thing, gold casing and pearly tooth, could fit easily on my pinkie fingernail, yet so powerful that it could elicit a flinch—a flinch with the ability to bring forth the self-consciousness in me that, only shallowly buried, seems always lying in wait.

The Magician

ONCE, AT AN APPOINTMENT WITH the hairdresser I had come to think of as the "Magician" because of the magic he wielded with his scissors, I coughed. I was getting over a mild cold and still had the occasional dry cough—more of a clearing of the throat, really, than a full-blown, mucousy affair. As I first sat down in the salon chair, eager for the cut that I'd scheduled weeks in advance, I coughed one of those small and, to me, inoffensive coughs.

At the sound, the Magician, who was at that moment inspecting my loosened hair, jumped away from me. His hand flew to his face, fingers shielding his nose and mouth.

"Do you have a cold?" he demanded, suddenly serious.

"No, not really . . . I mean, I had a small one last week."

His shoulders relaxed minutely as he cautiously drew his hand from his face. "Okay, because I *cannot* get a cold."

As he spoke, I was reminded of the intensifying fact of AIDS, and that certain men in San Francisco were in danger of dying of pneumonia. But this was not my reality, and what I had been focused on all that day was the fact that I really wanted my hair cut. I had waited weeks, and today, the day of my appointment, I had filled my car with gas, driven south across the Golden Gate, paid the bridge toll, navigated the steep hills and one-way streets that define the city, circled and re-circled the block until I found a parking place, put the carefully collected coins in the meter, and walked to the salon; the last thing I wanted was to wait another month or so.

Also, I truly believed I wasn't contagious.

"What if I cover my mouth?" I suggested.

I sat for the rest of the appointment holding a small towel to my face. The Magician and I exchanged commentary now and then about small nothings, but he reserved his real conversation for people more interesting to him than a young woman, heterosexual and shy of him, harking from the northern suburbs across the bridge. Probably due to my cough and its psychological repercussions, he chatted companionably with the stylist working next to us, another gay man, about death. "I've already been to fifty funerals this *year*," he confessed.

Friends, former boyfriends, ex-lovers, all of them were dying. Medical science still lagged behind this reality. Reagan's government had only exacerbated the crisis with its dismissal of the disease as one belonging to a lower strata, the dregs of society—the corrupt and sinful "homosexuals."

What wasn't really familiar to me, back then, seems very familiar to me now. Sitting on a styling chair in that hair salon, I came to realize—intellectually, theoretically—the source of his fear, his fear of contagion, of germs, of death. But I didn't *feel* it like I do now, having since lived two years of shutdowns and masking and impatient waiting for effective vaccines. This man, this "Magician," I imagine, was also waiting impatiently, desperately so, for the magic of science: a pill, a vaccine, a cure. His magic, his skill set and his art, could not guarantee him safety and longevity.

"*SABES*," SAID MY MOTHER IN Spanish, her voice low and tone serious, "*cuando era jovencito, mi primo Miguel* was infected by an older man he met in Canada." She didn't mean infected by HIV or AIDS, unheard of then, but by homosexuality. This quiet story about one of her many first cousins was meant as a warning, a dark fairy tale. *Beware: Homosexuality is contagious.* I was not a boy, yet she still found it necessary to tell me this cousin's fate. Perhaps she wanted to keep me from ever associating with people not "*finos*," not classy—those she considered perverse, obscene, lost.

I was brought up by a mother who was herself brought up in mid-twentieth-century Peru within an extended family of devout Catholics. In her world, homosexuality wasn't discussed out loud, only whispered about in the worst kind of gossip or as a warning. Homosexual men were called "*maricones*" and considered a rare, mutated species: unfortunate deviations from her understanding of heterosexual masculinity.

DURING THE SAME ERA AS my visit to the Magician's salon, when I was in my early twenties, I entered a hospital for a routine doctor's appointment. As I walked through the lobby to the elevators, I passed a figure I will never forget. A man stood, straight and erect, with the help of a silver-topped cane. He was tall and thin, impossibly so—emaciated. Everything about him shrieked AIDS: the hollows under his sharp cheekbones, his sunken eyes, the veins on his forehead visible in blue, his slim hips, from which hung expensive designer denim. He was wealthy—his look, even his bearing, exuded the power and authority of money. In addition to the designer denim, he wore a thick leather jacket, soft and supple, over a quality and expertly ironed button-down shirt. On one wrist he wore a silver chain, heavy and finely worked. He still had a full head of silvery hair on his bony skull, evocative of a once robust, now degraded virility. And despite his skeletal frame, he emanated a quiet dignity as he stood there alone, most likely waiting for his ride.

I was left feeling a sense of tragedy: He was dying, and all his money and possessions, all his connections, could not save him.

LAST WEEKEND I TRAVELED WITH my husband by plane from San Francisco to Calgary for the eightieth birthday celebration of one of the last three family survivors of my mother's generation.

This cousin, similar to Miguel, relocated as a young man to Canada for work. During the party at a golf club in the city suburbs, I talked with one of his daughters. Somehow, we ended up discussing Miguel. She had intimate knowledge of his history, whereas I had only the strange, sad story from my mother. She'd grown up close to him, and knew him as her beloved "Tío."

"He would pick me up at kindergarten and pretend he was kidnapping me," she told me. "My teacher would always roll her eyes and say, 'We already know you're picking up your niece today. You're on the list!'" She also told me about her parents hosting him on the couch in their living room in the last months of his life, after he was weakened by AIDS.

When I asked if he had a partner, a life companion, she said many of his exes had come to the funeral, some of whom she'd known and liked, but he'd had no single, enduring love.

IT IS THE 2010S. I STAND AT a party with a group of people I don't know. This is more than thirty years after my visits to the Magician, well after the brief dream of free and unfettered sex, of open and validated bonds between men, and then the deaths of hundreds of thousands of those men because of that dream.

We've formed a small circle of about five, most of us with drinks in our hands; I'm in high heels and a pencil skirt, holding a glass of red wine. A man in his early sixties, wearing a trendily fitted suit and colorful dress shirt, holds court; he has the confident affect of the dryly witty, of someone who knows he's entertaining, that he can hold attention without much effort. He's telling a story, and we all listen, hanging on his every word.

He's talking about his past as a young man in San Francisco. He tells us about the paradise the city was then for men like him, for him and his friends and his lovers. The paradise of a city they could call home, of streets and neighborhoods they could call theirs, of dancing and parties and sex. Until, that is, people started getting sick: their condition—fatigue, weight loss, bruises, and sores—a mystery. Then the deaths from this condition, ignored by the government even after their cause was identified.

This man, however, began to feel lucky. When some years passed and he didn't get sick, he started to believe that somehow, someway, he had escaped. Until the day he tested positive.

"I had an appointment with a doctor," he says, "to discuss my results. I waited in the examining room, scared out of my wits. I knew I was going to receive a death sentence."

As he speaks I imagine a younger version of this man, a scared and vulnerable version of this funny, sarcastic man, sitting on the crinkly tissue covering the examination table in a sterile doctor's office, looking at his hands so he would not have to see the posters on the wall or the brochures in their display cases detailing contagion and disease, support groups and grief therapy, the necessary protection he had neglected to use—not knowing what was coming, the virus that would bring with it the deaths of beloved friends and partners.

This man tells us about waiting for the doctor to walk into the room where he sat alone—dreading her appearance, fearing the answer to his question: *How much time do I have?*

But then, in a matter of minutes, his life pivoted once again. The young doctor informed him that actually, no, he wasn't going to die anytime soon of AIDS. She told him about a new treatment, a new cocktail of drugs, a newly approved regimen that promised to prolong life indefinitely for patients sick like him, for bodies infected like his.

"I literally had a new lease on life—I walked out with all of the rest of my life ahead of me. I wasn't going to die, I was going to live."

The joy is palpable in his voice, on his face, as he stands at this cocktail party and tells his tale to his rapt listeners. I can see that he still exists in the light-filled prism of that moment when he moved from the cage of certain and impending death to the freedom of suddenly expanded time. He had spent agonizing hours, days, weeks believing that he was doomed, that he was sentenced to an imminent death, that he was going to be one of the tens of thousands in San Francisco who would die too early, one of the hundreds of thousands across the country who would die too young. Then, instead of that one desperately short and narrow path left before him, he had, once again, an open vista, the breadth and depth of the horizon—what many of us take for granted until we can't.

I AM SEVENTEEN YEARS OLD AND at a crowded club near Haight-Ashbury. All around me are men. Mostly young, some a bit older. They dance together, or next to each other, or seemingly alone. But they all dance.

The club was in San Francisco, and I only went one time, with a small group of girlfriends. I remember the rough, still-to-be-gentrified neighborhood, the dark street close to midnight, and the dim interior, a big, unadorned space with every visible surface painted black. What brought us there that night? The music.

One man in particular stays in my memory even all these years later, as if I'm still looking at him, in the moment. He dances completely, all of himself concentrated in this act. He dances with someone, but I don't take note of his partner. This man is older than me but young, probably in his late twenties or early thirties. He is a man, not a boy, and he is buff. He obviously works out with weights. He wears denim, loosely fitted, low slung, perhaps even with the top of his briefs showing—which would be appropriate, because he looks like the Calvin Klein ad that will become famous some years later, a young and muscled Marky Mark dominating Times Square or staring out at us, his face serious and sexy at the same time, from the pages of countless magazines. The lights in this scene from my memory seem to shine exclusively on this one man, dancing so intently and yet so naturally, looking so handsome and seeming so happy; on his body, so muscled and shaved smooth; on the denim that is so perfect both on his hips and in this setting.

No one notices us, the young women, still girlish with our full cheeks, with our dramatic makeup and trendy, cobbled-together outfits, with our high expectations for adventure in what we have always considered our city. No one notices me at all, for I am invisible here. I'm like the proverbial fly on the wall, small and insignificant in this environment yet looking, watching, observing.

My girlfriends and I are the only women in the entire venue. We walk around, squeezing past sweaty dancers who don't acknowledge our presence by glance or expression. We don't factor into their night, their mood, their club, their community.

It feels strange to me, a young woman, having already become accustomed to looks and overtures from men just because I am young and female. In this space, my friends and I, despite our carefully chosen outfits, our makeup and hair gel, our lipstick and cigarettes, are desexualized. But I don't resent this. We've come, after all, primarily for the music.

Regardless of that strange new feeling in that brave new world that I somehow stumbled into, I always have in my memory of my past clubbing in San Francisco, smoking and drinking and trying to look cool, the image of that one man—so complete and sufficient in his person, his sexuality, his pleasure—dancing, half naked, in the light that seemed to shine only for him.

A FRIEND OF MINE (A GAY MAN) to whom I have recounted this story of the dancer in that club long ago says it sounds like I was looking at penguins in a zoo. That I was a voyeur of sorts, fascinated with the "Other," by this subculture so different from my own. He tells me too, though, that he knows I'm not judgmental of homosexuality, its identity or lifestyle. But he thinks my memories seem one-sided, perhaps exoticizing the men I observed as different and alien.

His opinion floods me with self-doubt. Am I the problem? Are my memories? Or is it the way I relate them?

MY FRIEND'S PENGUIN COMMENT reminds me of a June day, long ago, when my grandmother was visiting us in California for several weeks and my mother decided it would be interesting to drive to the perimeter of the Pride Parade taking place in San Francisco one sunny weekend. Thinking back to that afternoon in the city, when we watched the parade from our parked car, it seems clear to me that, especially for my mother and grandmother, our outing resembled a tour of a zoo. But instead of us walking from exhibit to exhibit, the "penguins" paraded past the spectators. My grandmother marveled at the proud men and women marching, some wearing what for her amounted to bizarre costumes—frills and boas and (only) leather chaps, biker jackets and dog collars and platform heels.

Later, on our drive home back across the bridge, my grandmother shook her head and said what we'd just seen was a "*Sodoma y Gomorra.*" Yet in my memory of her judgment there's also a small smile on her face, an upturn at the corner of her mouth, a crinkling at the edges of her eyes. She seemed to condemn, as would an Old Testament patriarch, but somehow this condemnation was undermined by her tone and expression—by, ultimately, her obvious enjoyment of the afternoon.

So what about me? I'm the one, after all, grappling today with my memories, with my perspective on an "other" subculture, one not mine, but influential in my understanding of those not like me. My memory of that afternoon is mostly of watching my grandmother watching the parade. I too, of course, was fascinated by the colors and the outfits and the sometimes defiant, sometimes humorous banners and signs. I also was taken aback by naked backsides, violent-looking chains, leashes, spikes. Even by hairy muscled legs teetering on impossibly high heels and huge, synthetic wigs. I hadn't yet learned to see the parade as a display of exuberance, a celebration of the positive, proud manifestation of the self. I was, in my late teens, largely a product of six years in conservatively Catholic countries, four years at an evangelical missionary middle school, and four years at a Dominican high school for girls. Yet at the same time I was trying to make sense of both what I saw and how those I loved reacted, while keeping these observations in my memory to analyze later. Could this have been a step in my becoming more self-aware?

I MET RICHARD THROUGH LAURENCE, whom I met at a Talk Talk concert in San Francisco one early summer night in the late eighties. It was a small affair held in an intimate venue, where chatting with fellow trendy attendees was fairly easy. Laurence, slight of build and quiet of manner, he of the jaunty sailor cap and occasional blue-and-white striped shirt, was the more damaged of the two friends. Richard would tell me months after we met that Laurence often took to the streets late at night—Polk or Castro, usually—desperate to lose his pain in anonymous sex. Richard shook his head, his lips pursed and eyes worried but his tone frustrated. "It's so sad, so dangerous," he said. "I don't know how to help him."

Over time I became closer to Richard, probably because he was more open, more gregarious and gossipy, than the reserved Laurence. One Saturday night that turned into early Sunday morning, I drove my wide, bench-seat sedan from a club to an after-party with Richard next to me and other clubbing acquaintances in the back. When we arrived at the apartment building where the after-party was being held, my back seat emptied of passengers, but for some reason Richard and I stayed in the car. Was he already asleep at that point, his head on my lap? Or did he fall asleep mid-conversation, his head slowly finding its way between my torso and the steering wheel?

What I do remember very clearly is that he fell asleep at some point, deeply and trustfully, lying on my lap in the front seat of my car.

I sat there, surrounded by the still, early morning darkness in front of an apartment building, other parked cars around me, a streetlamp or two the only light. The radio was on, turned as always to The Quake, the one "alternative" station at the time in San Francisco, where I had listened to Talk Talk in the first place. I wanted to go into the party, to join the others, including those who had already left the car. But I had Richard's unconscious head on my lap, vulnerable and innocent.

I waited some more. Minutes crawled by. Did I smoke a cigarette? There were no cell phones or Wi-Fi, no easy access to news, social media, games, apps, videos, texts, or email.

What was my breaking point? Commercials on the radio? A sore back? Boredom? In any case, I finally tired of my vigil as Richard's soft pillow, and carefully lifted his head with one hand to slide out from under him. I left the keys inside the car, and locked the doors so he would be safe. Then I joined the party.

Some minutes later, Richard burst into the apartment to find me among the other after-partiers and accused me of abandoning him. I defended my actions, saying I didn't want to wake him, but he never really forgave me. It's always been a source of guilt for me, despite my good intentions. I knew that both Richard and Laurence were children rejected by their parents because of their sexuality, ejected from the home to survive on their own. They'd made it to San Francisco, where there were like-minded people, but their life was still a daily struggle to pay rent, eat, survive. They formed surrogate families, and maybe Richard saw me as a sort of family member who had once again rejected him, this time by leaving him alone inside a car in an unfamiliar neighborhood, only the darkness around him.

BEFORE WE LEFT CALGARY AND my Canadian relatives, my husband and I decided to take a quick road trip through Banff to Lake Louise. We'd been there once before—twenty-two years earlier, to be exact—with our first son and my family.

Fortunately, given the amount of tourist buses, campers, cars, and vans trying to crowd into the two parking lots by the lake, I'd reserved a table for lunch at the Fairmont's Lakeside

Restaurant prior to our journey. We were ushered through a separate and empty lane to the hotel's private parking garage. After walking a few yards, we entered a lobby luxurious with plush carpet, chandeliers, and a huge vase of freshly cut flowers. It was a sunny day, warm but not hot, a bit hazy from nearby wildfires but not smoky. The lake's waters were a cool light blue. The mountain range loomed up and away from the lake's edge, a snowy frame. It was just as stunning a sight as I remembered.

Our waitress guided us to our table on the patio right next to a low wall set with planters of cheerful red geraniums. It seemed ideally positioned, but when my husband excused himself to use the bathroom, I looked around me and questioned my initial satisfaction. Behind us was a table placed against the restaurant's windows so that the two men sitting at it side by side could look over our table, the low wall, and the rows of flowers directly at the sky and the lake and the mountains. I pondered our relative positions vis-à-vis the view. Could theirs be better?

As I pondered, I noticed that the men, a middle-aged couple simply yet elegantly garbed—suede loafers, slim trousers, clean haircuts—were preparing to leave. As they began to step away, I stood to test their seats against mine.

One of them gestured toward their table. "Are you planning to move? It's a great view."

I smiled my assent, and as they walked away and I approached their seats, he turned back briefly to say, "Enjoy."

By the time my husband returned from the bathroom, I had transferred our menus, water glasses, and napkins to the table bequeathed to us by the men. He saw at a glance the advantage of my move and settled down beside me facing the view framed by columned arches. We sat there for more than an hour, eating lunch and drinking cups of tea as we enjoyed our improved vantage point.

Death of a Patriarch

IN THE HOT WIND WE CONGREGATED, all of us who had come to mourn a patriarch, a husband, a father, a father-in-law, a compatriot, a friend. We gathered together, dressed in black, those of us who had come to receive his body and position it in the grave, or to throw a handful of dirt onto the corpse, or to recite from the Quran, or to weep and keen, or to remember and regret, or to wait until after the family left to shovel in the remaining soil and maneuver the heavy concrete top over the hole.

We stood on the barren ground, a lonely area in San Francisco's East Bay surrounded by hills and meadows, rimmed by yellow grass. Nearby, the freeway droned. The wind itself seemed to carry with it a sense of death and despair, of fatalism and endings, of global warming and climate change. The sense of desolation I felt standing at my father-in-law's funeral, baking in the heat and irritated by the grit of the blowing dust while holding a black parasol over my mother-in-law's coiffured head, was only reinforced by the haphazard rectangles of artificial turf on the graves, graves that I knew hid the remains of real people, beloved mothers and fathers, sons and daughters, sisters and brothers, aunts and uncles and cousins and friends.

Like a crow in the bleak landscape, I clustered with the others around the grave. My mother-in-law's elegant parasol, purchased decades earlier in Paris, looked weirdly incongruous in its modish sophistication. We stood in the windswept clearing among other flat graves, some sporting small slabs of granite perched at their heads with names shallowly etched in a metallic silver or gold. At that moment I felt an acute nostalgia for the Victorian graveyards I grew up reading about in books, the ones beside quaint stone churches, covered in moss and ivy, individual names and personal epitaphs carefully carved on heavy headstones, graveyards that, as the resting places for the dead, felt peaceful—snug and familiar. We had visited my British ancestors' graveyard earlier that year on a family vacation, and the differences I couldn't help but note now intensified my current discomfort in this arid setting. I compared the lush greens with the bleached yellows, the marble headstones aged into picturesqueness with the slick, square slabs of granite; I saw how my memory of the decades-old trees, oak and elm and chestnut, which lent charming shadow to the garden of graves, clashed with my present vision of a lone pair of struggling saplings bending in the hot wind and failing to give shade to even one plot; I noticed the difference between the plants flourishing in the damp English earth, climbing up fence and wall and gravestone alike, and the plastic pots of fake flowers tilting on the uneven surface of these gravesites by a motorway.

Here in the glare of the sun, with no clouds, no trees, and no shade, I was exposed, like a skeleton left to the elements in an indifferent desert. At this burial ground I felt trapped in a Salvador Dalí painting, alienated by the flat, hard ground, the cement sides of the narrow cavity, and the small bulldozer waiting nearby to finish the job of covering the body with practical finality.

Minutes earlier, the plain white van had pulled up, stark and utilitarian, with no sense of tradition, of gravitas and solemnity. The cardboard coffin had been taken out of the back of the van by mosque men who, at the appropriate moment, opened it to remove the linen-shrouded body. They handed it, as planned beforehand, to my husband and his brother, to the sons of my father-in-law, who took it, careful with respect and love, in their outstretched arms, and together laid it gently, face toward Mecca in the East, at the bottom of the grave in which they were standing.

I watched as they both—dressed impeccably in dark suits, timeless and formal in leather shoes and belts, ties and cuff links—lowered themselves, as per Muslim custom, into the trench that had been designated as their father's final resting place. At first I'd felt uneasy with the spectacle of my husband climbing down into a dirt hole, of the father of my children descending into the ground. But then, as I watched him reach out for his father, sharing his heft and weight with his brother, and saw the gentleness with which they held him, I felt only the beauty of children being the last to handle a parent's body, to lay it down to rest, to say goodbye with their tenderness and their touch.

That morning I kept my own young children from their grandfather's funeral at the mosque in Livermore that the family, not having a community mosque nearby in Palo Alto, had contacted for the service. I wanted to shelter my sons, to protect them, to keep sad or disturbing images from taking hold forever in their memories—so I left them with my mother and attended the service with my mother-in-law and sister-in-law, standing and kneeling and praying in the soundproof room behind the section reserved for the men and the imam. I wanted to stand by my husband as a companion in mourning, but instead found myself playing that role for his mother. I looked through the thick glass partition separating the men from the women and watched the cardboard coffin being passed from man to man to land at the front as the imam spoke a eulogy and the congregation rose and sat, worshipped and prayed together. I followed the movements of my mother-in-law, mimicking her as she stood and knelt and held out her hands, palms up, to her god.

The atmosphere in the women's section, unlike the men's, was casual and relaxed: Toddlers played with their toys and little girls and boys ran about at will. Babies slept or fussed and mothers called to their children. Part of me enjoyed the warmth and intimacy that came with this informality, while another resented the quiet seriousness that was taken for granted for the men, a solemnity that contrasted with the constant distraction deemed natural for the women.

The day before, my husband and brother-in-law had left together for the morgue to be coached by an imam through the ritual cleansing of the paternal body. I myself saw it, but only afterward, when it had been washed and prepared for burial in a simple white shroud and placed in its cardboard box, looking shrunken and diminished. My mother-in-law, overcome with sadness and stress as we gazed at the corpse—this foreign, unrecognizable figure—faltered where she stood, almost falling to the ground. I rushed to hold her up and squeezed her shoulders tightly as if to say, *I am here, you are not alone, you will be okay, this too shall pass*. At that moment I wondered why I—the daughter-in-law, the non-blood relation, the non-Muslim, the non-Syrian—was the one performing this duty and not my husband or his brother, not the widow's own beloved sons. I could only think that they, weighed down with their own grief, could not support their mother in hers.

The evening before I had realized that the widow should not be left alone that night, the first night after my father-in-law had drawn his last breath and been taken away hours later by the coroners in black plastic, the sound of the long zipper closing over his face making death real. When I shared my concern with my brother-in-law, he reassured me that of course he would stay with his mother so she would not feel alone. But when the time came for us to say good night, I saw my brother-in-law depart with his wife and daughters for his own home a few minutes away and understood that I was the only one left to comfort my mother-in-law, to make sure that she did not sleep alone in the dark master bedroom, on the empty marital bed, in the room that she had shared for decades with her husband, the same room where her husband had died just hours before. My own husband had already announced his plan to go upstairs to bed, upstairs to where his children lay sleeping, protected from the sight and sounds of their grandfather's death and their grandmother's grief. I understood my husband's need for that separation, his need to get away from the bedroom where he had stayed faithfully for hours before and after his father died.

"Do you want me to stay with you tonight?" I asked my mother-in-law tentatively; we were alone together for the first time after my brother-in-law closed the front door behind him and my husband climbed the stairs to join his sons in their sleep.

"Oh, would you?" she responded. "I would be most grateful to you!" My mother-in-law, speaking English as a second language and educated as a doctor in England, still retained a formal syntax even after forty years in California.

So that is how I found myself lying in the bed of my parents-in-law, trying to fall asleep where my father-in-law used to sleep, feeling the hollow in the mattress carved out over the years by the weight of his large, heavy body. Thankfully, I kept reminding myself as I stared into the darkness, acutely aware of my mother-in-law's breathing, my father-in-law hadn't actually died in that bed, in the same exact place where I now lay. Finally, I came up with a way to mitigate the awkwardness of sleeping beside my mother-in-law—the mother-in-law who had, in the early years of my marriage to her son, been reserved and cold, who had failed to welcome me into the family, who had not wanted her son to marry me, who had judged me for years, who had constantly compared me to a Syrian, Muslim, Arabic-speaking ideal. I went upstairs myself and brought my younger son down to sleep in the middle of the bed, in between me and his grandmother. It soothed me to have him there with me, his breathing steady as he slept.

Before that I had seen my father-in-law just two hours after he died—in his bedroom, on an emergency cot, the sound of the Quran being sung playing throughout. This was a sound I had learned to find soothing and always found hauntingly beautiful. It comforted me to know that he died surrounded by that sound, those words, that music. His body then was still big and sturdy and robust. His skin still olive and his face still ruddy. His hands wide, his limbs full. He lay on his last bed, the wheeled hospital cot that had been brought in for his final days and placed next to the side of the bed he had slept in for over four decades.

I had walked in, after sending my children straight to sleep, and joined my husband in his vigil beside his father. My husband sat on a chair pulled up to the cot, or stood looking down at the body, wiping away tears and murmuring prayers as he massaged his father's feet, rubbed his legs, squeezed his hands and arms, smoothed his hair off his forehead, kissed his brow, spoke his love to him. We stood vigil thus, the elder son saying his goodbyes through caress and prayer and I, the daughter-in-law, witnessing him with the body of his father, listening to the melodic recitation of the Quran, holding the back of my husband, the grief-stricken son.

Only hours earlier, I'd been sitting in a local French bistro celebrating my own father's eighty-third birthday. I sat with my family: both parents, my brother and sister, and my two children. My husband had driven south to his parents' house several hours prior, called home to be with his father, the father who had been dying for a few weeks but who today, tonight, might really go. With somewhat of a "just in case" mentality, with sadness tinged with resignation, my husband got into his car alone to make the long drive from our town to his parents', a drive that took him over the Golden Gate Bridge, past Alcatraz, through San Francisco, by missions and reservoirs. I stayed behind, all of us uncertain as to the timing of the course of events and wanting to celebrate my father's continued life on his birthday.

I was sitting on the banquette, sandwiched between my children, a son on each side, talking over poached salmon and wild rice, when my cell phone vibrated on the table beside me. I snatched it up right away, on high alert for news from my husband about his father, and listened intently, holding the phone tight to my ear against the noisy hum of the restaurant.

It had happened. The patriarch and the grandfather, the father and the husband—my father-in-law—was dead.

Silver Street

My aunt and mother and I sat around the breakfast table in my aunt and uncle's San Isidro apartment. We'd just finished our café con leche and fresh mangoes. My aunt had an intriguing way of serving the fruit: She first took her time peeling away the skin, then cut the remaining mound of flesh into neat cubes to be forked into the mouth with ease. Although I was a grown woman, my way was far messier—I tore the peel off with my fingers and then sliced off the flesh in quick strips as close to the pit as I could, which made for much dripping of juice and waste of fruit. But I've always been impatient, not only physically but also mentally, jumping to conclusions, making quick assumptions.

That morning we were planning our day, which included a trip to the jewelry store. This particular boutique, located off downtown Lima's Avenida La Paz (which I called the "Silver Street" because of its blocks of silver stores), offered custom designs as well as necklaces, rings, bracelets, and cuffs already crafted in both silver and gold, gleaming brightly in their polished glass cabinets. My mother had several gold pieces she wanted refashioned, including a couple of rings that had to be sized for my sister's slightly larger fingers, a bracelet that needed to be made smaller, and a gold necklace she wished melted down and made into a second bracelet.

"¿Vamos a la joyería de los hermanos?" asked one sister of the other.

"Sí, hay que darle negocio al jorobadito."

Jorobadito means "little hunchback." My Peruvian relatives, especially my aunt and sometimes my mother, often patronized certain people by infantilizing them. Everyone did this, as it is a common way of speaking in South America, but coming from my aunt, who was an unapologetic snob, it always felt more patronizing. In this case, one of the brothers who owned this establishment off Avenida La Paz apparently had a curved back.

I didn't think much of her comment at that moment in the kitchen as I stood to clear the table from the breakfast detritus of used plates and emptied coffee cups. But it clearly had lodged itself in my brain, for when we finally left for the shop, all I could think about was *el jorobado* and what he would look like. The romance of that figure, culminating in the legendary Quasimodo as the indentured laborer and hopeless lover, played in the background of my mind.

Avenida La Paz isn't the safest of streets; the storefronts have folded iron gates that close at night, and padlocks and chains are de rigueur. When my aunt dropped us off near the entrance to our destination, opting to wait in a nearby parking space rather than leave her car vulnerable to vandalism or theft, my mother admonished me to walk quickly and keep my purse close. At one point in between my aunt's car and the storefront, a group of young men sporting black tattoos and tough attitudes approached and my mother pulled me into the nearest shop entrance to pretend we had business there, wary of passing these youthful thugs on the open sidewalk.

That day, as usual, Silver Street was busy and crowded. The shops of antiques and precious metals seemed stuffed into their small spaces along each side of the thoroughfare. I was reminded of the story of Atahuallpa, who, for his own ransom, appealed to the greed of the Spanish conquistadores by having his people fill two rooms from floor to ceiling with gold and silver. Precious objects came from all over the Incan Empire, but Pizarro merely took the spoils and executed the emperor anyway. Although I'd never been to the jorobado's workshop, I had visited Avenida La Paz with my mother and aunt many times and it had always seemed to me as if block after block, store after store, room after room was filled with precious objects—gold and silver, gems and pearls. In silver there were baroque candelabras, vases of all sizes and shapes, and massive, ornate frames. People walked up and down the sidewalks, but with purpose rather than for entertainment. There were more men than women, and they strode about going to and from their business.

I don't know if it was because of my mother's multiple warnings, but I felt danger lurking as we navigated our way around the different stores. There was just so much silver and gold, so many objects that could translate into monetary wealth. In most of the shops the decorated urns, the gleaming candlesticks, the antique cuffs and chokers seemed crowded in display windows, with little attention to effect. Only a few of the stores, the higher-end ones, had stylish window displays with attention clearly given to artful spacing. I looked at the men walking to and fro with suspicion: Who might be illegitimate? Who might be scouting the stores for illegal purposes? The broken promises of the conquistadores, the brutal colonization by the Europeans, still manifested themselves here through the riches reserved entirely for the higher classes. There seemed to be so much wealth in the crafted objects easy for the physical taking—how could it exist, day after day, without tempting the abject poor (of whom there were many in this city) to steal it by force or stealth? I was highly conscious of my own affluence; having risked bringing a handbag, I tucked it more firmly under my arm, at the same time turning the gold lock of my leather cuff toward the inside of my wrist so that a random glimmer wouldn't tempt a thief. Worried about being targeted as a rich tourist, I tried to look businesslike and at ease, as if I belonged there.

Unlike me, my mother had visited the shop run by the two brothers before, as was evidenced that day by her confident beeline toward an inconspicuous entrance to an even more inconspicuous alley. As we entered the narrow passageway, the noise and activity of the street faded away behind us. The alley was quiet and seemed to serve as a conduit for different doors, a couple of which looked residential.

The first we passed was the official storefront, which, although opened to the public with lights on inside, remained protected by the iron bars of the folding gates. We didn't pause to window-shop through those bars; instead, we continued our purposeful walk along the narrow corridor, which had now started to twist and turn.

I looked around me as I followed my mother, trying to observe as much as possible. I could see a sliver of blue sky compressed above me by the upper stories of the buildings around us that could have been either houses or storerooms. I could hear disembodied twitters and trills, and I imagined we were passing hidden courtyards with fountains surrounded by ferns and birds, proof of the Moorish influence that had crossed the Atlantic with the explorers.

At this point we walked single file, my mother and I, in the way of mama ducks and their ducklings. She was the leader and, when I thought about it, she was the One, with a capital *O*, upon whom I had imprinted at birth like a duckling—love at first sight. Thus, although already in my early fifties, it made sense that I would follow her without question while navigating this unfamiliar maze of corridors toward, for me, the unknown. We were on a quest, and she was my fearless guide. We had come bearing gold and diamonds in hopes of having them transformed by the magic of the jorobado and his brother.

My mother navigated the eerie labyrinth by instinct and I followed, suspending my disbelief in our safety. The alley was getting narrower, the mix of unfinished concrete and brick walls around us taller, more broken glass and pointed iron guarding against intruders. A mop leaned against a door and a box of Ajax sat beside it; the walls were rough concrete, the tiles below my feet cracked. I held my arms close to my sides, stepping carefully, not because I was scared right then of pickpockets or muggers but because I didn't want to brush inadvertently against a grimy wall or step in a puddle of murky liquid.

The sky was by then invisible, all sounds muted; it would have been impossible to know or even guess that this place existed from the street outside. I could have been in a surrealist dream, unmoored and disoriented, unsure of my bearings save for the beacon that was my mother as she walked directly in front of me. Although eighty-five, her walk was not yet a shuffle, and her back had barely begun the curve into the downward gaze of the elderly.

After what seemed to me a long time, we stopped at a door, nondescript save for the many locks that lined one side. My mother knocked, and after a short while the locks began to click open from the inside.

Having already romanticized *el jorobado* in my mind since hearing of him earlier that morning, I was anxious to see who would be at the door. The long walk in silent passageways into the unknown recesses of the city block, into what felt like a hidden place, a secret spot, had only intensified the mystery around our mission.

When the door opened after much turning of keys and sliding of bolts, I couldn't get a clear glimpse of the man who opened it because I was following so closely behind my mother. She, in turn, followed behind our host after quick greetings on each of their parts. He led us from a cramped entryway into a larger room, one lit rather dimly by artificial light, for there were no windows. The walls were pale and dingy; a furnace held court on one side, and shelves with steel and iron instruments decorated the other. I settled precariously on a rickety stool, thighs tensed to prevent an unexpected wobble from depositing me on the dirty floor. My mother sat near me at the center of the room, next to a black contraption that turned out to be an anvil.

Before I sat down on my stool I had seen that behind me was a framed image, high up on the wall in what might have been a place of honor, as it alone faced the room from the otherwise blank space. It was a photograph of a pope, not Pope Francis, toward whom I had such warm feelings because of his humility and compassion, but an earlier pope, Pope Benedict XVI. Over his head was the image of the perennially young Jesucristo, pale-skinned and light-eyed. His presence seemed a benevolent one; his face looked kind and forgiving. Gold rays emanated from him to surround the pope. This picture felt like a kind of Catholic talisman, a protective artifact, comparable to the evil eye I'd seen everywhere in Turkey. Yet the room itself reminded me of Hawthorne's depiction of Aylmer's dungeon-like laboratory, where his assistant Aminadab toils all day and night, the only light coming from torches and the fire that continuously heats an iron cauldron. Adding its own dimension to the scene was the Andean flute music I could hear playing from some invisible radio in a separate room.

I took all this in as we entered the room, as I was invited to sit down, as I seated myself on the wooden stool, as my mother sat down next to me beside the anvil, as the business talk began between my mother and the person who had opened the door. It was only then, as their consultation began, that I started to look closely at this man. I stared at him whenever he turned from us to pick up something, a measuring tool or a small digital scale. When he turned back in our direction, I quickly averted my gaze to look elsewhere: over his shoulder, to the side, at my hands that held my purse on my lap.

Multiple times during their conversation, my mother asked for my advice. *¿Qué crees que debemos hacer con esta pulsera?* Or *¿Te parece bien agrandar este anillo?* I'd then focus on her and the jewelry she had taken out of her bag. She asked me if my sister would like a certain bracelet if it were made smaller, or if her ring finger was in fact a size *siete* rather than *seis y medio*. I was irritated that my mother hadn't asked my sister these questions directly before we made the journey to this cave-like room, carefully carrying our precious cargo. But I tried to answer to the best of my knowledge, not wanting to feel like a little girl again, as I always did when I snapped at my mother: *Why didn't you ask her before we left? Well, why didn't you write it down so you wouldn't forget?* Then, when it was safe to do so once again, when our host's attention moved away from me and toward a ring, weighing it, or a bracelet, measuring it, I looked at him once more—at his height, at his gait when he walked a few short steps about the room, but mostly at his back. Was he *el jorobado*? Or was he the brother?

I remained ambivalent on this question for some time, as he didn't seem that short, and when he walked I thought I saw a slight limp, although I could have been imagining it. Finally, I believed I saw a small bump at the top of his back, starting at the base of his neck. Was this it, then? Was this El Jorobado de la Avenida La Paz whom I had been thinking about since we left San Isidro an hour before?

But then everything changed. Someone else came into the room. This person came in quietly, minding his own business, only nodding briefly at the man helping us. He was short, shorter than me, shorter than his brother. He had a full head of thick black hair and dark brown skin. But he also had a limp—one that, contrary to his brother's, was pronounced. And he had a hunched back. Unmistakable. It was this curvature, clearly, that caused the limp in his gait.

Everything about this man, the other brother, seemed to fit in with the room except for one thing: He had on a teal-blue Izod shirt. My eyes were drawn to this bright spot and I stared at him as he went to work at the stone furnace, his back to me, his eyes on the fire and the small welder he manipulated over a metal object. I couldn't see far enough to ascertain the nature of the object . . . Chain? Belt buckle? Jewelry box hinge?

I thought again about Aminadab, the Caliban figure in Hawthorne's story, yet this man's bright clean polo shirt (and his pleasant, albeit serious, face) kept resisting an identification with this type of figure. I was all set to complete my mental picture with a mythic character, yet I couldn't do it.

I did wonder, however, about his life up to this point. I guessed him to be in his late forties or early fifties. With Pope Benedict and Jesus behind me, I wondered if he was a virgin. Or perhaps that wasn't the case. I remembered then the boy from Cuenca to whom I had lost my own virginity. I remembered a story that he had told me, proud as a young peacock strutting his virility, about his adolescence. When he turned thirteen, his father had taken him to a brothel to be guided through the sex act for the first time by an expert. (I imagined the brothel stereotypically decorated in blood reds and lush velvets. I wondered if the father called ahead of time, being familiar with the madam of the establishment, and asked her to ready the gentlest and the prettiest of her stable of workers, similar to the selection of a mild, sweet horse for a beginning rider.) Apparently, this wasn't a strange and perverted ritual on the part of this particular father. This was fairly traditional.

Prostitutes were turned to so that young men might step forth into the world with confidence. Might this have happened to the jorobado? Or was this a classed tradition, in which only the more affluent boys, the ones destined to be doctors or diplomats or businessmen, had their sexual experience curated by their fathers?

I couldn't know the answers, but my mind continued to put forth possible scenarios as I watched him wield the torch expertly, wearing no helmet, gloves, or goggles.

He eventually left the workroom, as we also did a few minutes later when our business was done. On our way out of the alley I was attracted by the store that faced the street, the one with the glass cabinets displaying gleaming wares already shaped and buffed into beautiful art. Turning to my mother, I asked, "Can we look inside here for a bit?"

We'd emerged from the alley's mouth into the brightness of the sunny sky and the bustle of the crowded street.

"*¡Sí, vamos!*" My mother was always eager to shop, especially with one of her daughters, especially for the silver trays and vases and the gold jewelry she had grown up acquiring as must-haves for any woman of elegance and class.

The young shopkeeper hurried to unlock the chain and open the doors as we approached the store. She welcomed us in, smiling. She seemed to be about twenty-five years old, and she was pretty in a soft way—shiny brown hair, smooth olive skin, teeth straight and white. Her affect was the most attractive thing about her, though. She was friendly and professional, good-humoredly listening to my commentary and laughing at my jokes. I made conversation with her as I perused the wares displayed in the glass case between us. I found out she was educated, and that she had traveled to New York and Miami. Everything she said, every question she answered, was accompanied by a generous smile, her manner open and warm.

At one point I asked if I could order a certain bracelet in gold rather than the silver they had available, and she called out to a young man, *"Isaac, ven aquí porfa, ¿sabes si se puede hacer una pulsera como esta en oro?"*

Isaac was a tall and handsome young man, quieter than the young woman who was helping us but similarly well-mannered. Nosy as usual, I asked if she was related to him.

"Sí," she said, *"él es mi hermano."*

Wow, I thought to myself, *what a good-looking pair of siblings*. I'd already come to that point in my life where I delighted in youthful beauty, appreciating it for what it was instead of finding some fault with it as I had when young myself.

At one point, there was a question that neither brother nor sister could answer, and the young woman called out toward the back of the store, *"¡Papá!"*

I didn't have time to wonder who would emerge from the back of the store before I saw the bright blue shirt once again—the jorobado was her father. In an instant I realized I had to rework all of my assumptions, my imaginings of this man's past history and present situation. I had to revise the script, find a big, clean eraser and rub out all that I had written in my mind, in my usual rapid, impatient cursive, as the most likely of scenarios. The jorobado had a family—he had a wife and at least two gorgeous children, loyal to their parents, working together in the thriving family business. And to think that, just minutes ago, I'd pitied him for his lonely virginal existence, placing him in a small cell of a bedroom, sleeping nightly on a narrow cot, always alone.

Entrenched in inherited assumptions, blinded by stereotypes, I'd been utterly wrong. Our day of errands had started with notions of labyrinths and monsters, of quests and holy grails, or at least a version of the golden fleece. We'd driven from my aunt's apartment that morning on a mission for the metallurgic transformation made possible by a magician's skill—but instead it was I who, from that store full of shining silver and burnished gold, left transformed.

My Father's Walks

PICTURE THIS: A PHOTOGRAPH, looking to my eyes almost like a Polaroid in its small squareness, with its stark white border. Within the frame, however, is a scene of soft light and suffused warmth, a serenity still preserved after all these years by the picture's fading palette. At thirty, my mother sits in the yellowing grass of California's northern hills under the heavy branches of an oak tree. She sits demurely, legs to one side. Dressed in a simple cashmere sweater and capris, her black hair sounds the sole coquettish note as it falls seductively over one eye, a string of perfect pearls her only jewelry. She smiles tranquilly, her eyes clear and trusting.

My father, the person behind the camera, is courting my mother. For him, this courtship necessarily includes walking—hikes up mountains for picnics with a view, rambles on coastal beaches with sand rough underfoot, strolls down from Pacific Heights to the Marina's elegant promenade (runners and joggers are still decades from exercising along this long stretch of water). Although I can't see him, I know that behind the camera my father is tall and lean, handsome in a quiet dark-haired way: precise crew cut, smooth clean shave, plain flat-front khakis, simple polo shirt, a wristwatch his only adornment.

Two years later, my mother, pregnant and tired, trudges up the steep streets of San Francisco carrying groceries to her first apartment with my father. Although there is no photograph, I've been in that neighborhood of gracious mansions and small lush parks countless times; I know well the streets there that are so tilted the clutch of a stick shift induces panic, walking down them in heels is almost impossible, and walking up them feels like mountain climbing. My father resists buying a car—for him, walking is a quiet, dedicated passion.

The first years of their marriage my parents live in a stylish old-world apartment, its tall windows offering a view of the Golden Gate Bridge. There is a price to pay for all this beauty—the only way up and down their residential neighborhood without a car is by foot. My mother complains of overexertion, of fatigue. *Phoo,* her visiting mother-in-law says in her proper British accent, *exercise is good for you!* My father agrees, as he always does, with his mother.

Within a few weeks my mother miscarries. Devastated, she blames my father.

Seven years later, we—my parents, my little sister, my baby brother, and I—are temporary expats living in the Philippines. My father attempts family walks through the neighborhood, precursors to the daily excursions that become routine years later, back in the States. One evening, we are returning on foot to our house in a Manila suburb. The sky darkens dramatically in what feels like seconds. There is talk between my parents of an approaching storm and the need to hurry. They encourage my sister and me to quicken our steps as they accelerate their pace. We are still yards from our gate when thunder rumbles and it begins to rain. "Rain" in these tropics is an opening of the sky, a downpour of water, a release of heavy drops that splash thickly on pavement and gardens and houses alike. We break into a run, my father clutching my blanketed brother in both arms, my mother pulling at my sister's hand, all of us sprinting to the best of our abilities toward the shelter of the house. We arrive drenched, crowding into the front hallway to leave the monsoon raging outside.

Four years later, my family walks among the dozens of lofty eucalyptus trees that perfume the air up on a mountain ridge. We are still a young family, expats again, but now in Ecuador. My father has instated a tradition of twice-monthly walks through the country above our hillside home in Quito. Our walks have evolved, along with our growth as children, from random outings to planned expeditions. We protest often and loudly, but my father, a stubborn man, pays us no mind. Every other Sunday—without fail, rain or shine—we embark on what my siblings and I have dubbed the "cow pond" walk. We start off directly from our front door, leaving the house with a picnic lunch to eat once we've arrived at our destination.

To get to the pond we must walk through a poor community skirting our wealthy neighborhood. The handful of streets here are all dust and dirt; skeletal dogs roam around endlessly, seeking scraps of food; toddlers run about naked from the waist down, waiting, I assume, until they've been potty-trained for underpants; and women cleaning their homes empty buckets of brown water from second-story windows.

The pond itself is full of animal waste because cattle use this pond for hydration, plowing in, mindless of wet hooves, to drink and urinate at the same time. Because my father has decided on this spot to stop and rest beside the fetid water, we sit underneath a young eucalyptus and unwrap homemade sandwiches.

On our return, we must cross a small but deep canyon. A fall would most certainly result in broken bones, if not death. We use the makeshift bridge fashioned out of three long tree trunks, two bound together to walk along and another, slighter, suspended from rope as a railing. My father crosses twice before my siblings and I do, each time carrying one of our two dogs under an arm. Every time any one of us crosses, there is a sense of danger, of high risk, but my father insists that we do it nonetheless.

Three years later, settled back in California, my father dictates a daily constitutional, taken every evening after he arrives home from work and changes out of his suit and into his casual clothes. His children's complaints, especially mine, are vociferous and continuous. Sometimes, seeking to get the walk over with as soon as possible, I stride so quickly—steps long, arms pumping—that I resemble an Olympic power walker. Many evenings I outdistance my father in a few minutes, leaving him behind to proceed at his own deliberate pace. I ignore his suggestions to inhale deeply and "smell that fresh air," I deny his bids at conversation, I refuse to use this time to bond with my family.

One early morning during this period, my father drives our Plymouth Valiant, a wide sedan with a long bench as a back seat. There lies our dog, a husky-malamute mix that we adopted in Quito and brought with us when we returned to California. He is wounded, the deep red gash a vivid contrast against his white fur. He lies quietly, suffering silently, perhaps in shock—but then, he's always had a certain refined demeanor, an elegant poise. I try to comfort him from the front seat, periodically reaching back to pat his head. My father will drive to the vet after dropping me off at school.

Early this morning, a neighbor notified us that our dog was run over as he lay in the middle of the street, wanting to absorb the residual heat from the sun-warmed tarmac during the cold night. My father refuses to have him in the house—he does not believe in indoor pets—and despite his thick coat designed for the Arctic, our dog, feeling the increasing chill of a Northern California winter night, has learned to crawl under the fence to find a warm spot on the black asphalt beyond our yard.

Later today, I will learn that while I was in class my father watched my mother hold our dog in her arms as the vet injected his furry haunch. My father decided to put our dog down rather than risk a surgery that might leave him unable to walk again.

WHERE WAS MY MOTHER FOR many of these walks, these excursions on foot around the block or up a hill? It seems to me that when we lived in the United States she often recused herself from these ambulatory adventures of my father's. In not appreciating the daily constitutional as my father has always done so committedly, my mother is the opposite of her husband. I grew up between two extreme personalities, sometimes extreme in and of themselves, as individuals, but always extreme in comparison to one another. The personality differences that so polarized their interactions were informed by their individual upbringings. Thus there was the constant clashing of cultures in my home, within my family. My mother tells the story to this day of how she was so miserable the first year of her marriage to my father that she went to see a doctor. This psychiatrist, after hearing about her husband and their disagreements, advised, "Get a divorce."

My father grew up with walks—first in the parks and countryside of Germany, where he was born, then in France during the Second World War, and then continuing into adolescence, adulthood, and parenthood in the various places he lived around the world. Walking for my father is both relaxation and exercise, and because he is an addicted walkaholic, it must be a part of his every day. There's a line in one of my grandfather's diaries about my six-year-old father being punished that reads, "B was naughty this morning so he was left at home instead of going on our daily walk."

The antipathy my mother feels toward walking for walking's sake may have been reinforced by the uphill treks in the early days of her marriage and the consequent (in her eyes) miscarriage. It could also have been her upbringing, her culture, her particular sensibility as a young woman modeled and formed in Peru. "Fun" for my mother did not involve long hikes either on dirty trails or boring residential streets with Anglo Americans in what to her were scruffy, ugly clothes. For my mother, fun meant long luxurious lunches, beach outings in the dependable sun, and moonlit strolls surrounded by the scent of wisteria rather than a coerced march in awkward clothing, rain or shine, summer or winter, heat or chill.

Part of me believes that my mother enjoyed my father's family walks more when we lived abroad in Manila, Quito, or Rio de Janeiro. In these places, she was in her element. She never felt comfortable in the United States, finding the culture here too cold, too individualistic, too relentlessly serious and work-oriented. In Manila she joined us for walks occasionally, as she did that afternoon when the monsoon caught us outside. She also agreed once to drive hours into the country in order to take guided canoes before climbing to the top of a volcano to peer over the edge and see the roiling, red-hot lava center. This was all when my little brother was barely a few weeks old; I know this because there are photographs. Like the one of her courtship with my father under the oaks, where she's slim and svelte, smooth-haired and pearl-clad, there are two of her in this Philippines excursion, one in a canoe and a second standing at the edge of the rocky crater. Both of these later photographs depict a far less elegant scenario, however. In these my mother has just given birth a few weeks prior and she wears an A-line linen dress that has wrinkled many times over in the intense humidity. Her hair is similarly affected, and although it is scraped back, tendrils curl moistly around her forehead and on her neck. She looks exhausted. In the canoe, she's squished into the very bottom and holds my infant brother protectively in the crook of one arm while my toddler sister curls into the other.

Why agree to this adventure so soon after my brother was born? I can only assume she wanted to explore this interesting land with its Spanish colonial history and exotic terrain. She loves traveling and appreciates learning about any culture other than that of the United States. I think she agreed to this family trip because of her love of adventure in foreign lands combined with my father's pressuring enthusiasm for trekking up mountains. In Quito she'd sometimes join us on our weekend walks, even occasionally to the cow pond. And in Rio she never minded in the least our balmy evening walks by the beach to a restaurant.

Although my mother often clashed with my father over many things, she did understand him on a certain level. I remember an evening that seems so long ago now. We were in between stints abroad, after Manila and before Quito. My British grandmother was visiting us in California, staying with us in our tiny cottage with only one proper bedroom. Where did she sleep? I have no recollection whatsoever. Perhaps she slept in what was once the dressing room that was situated adjacent to the single bedroom in which we all—my mother, father, sister, brother, and I—slept in two beds pushed together.

On this particular evening, the lamps having just been turned on in the small living room, my grandmother received a long-distance phone call from Bethesda, where she lived with my grandfather. Her favorite sister, my father's aunt Mary, had died far away in England. My grandmother was quiet, and although I didn't see her cry, she was clearly distraught. My mother noticed, and she felt her mother-in-law's pain despite the deeply conflicted relationship she had with her. She said to my father, "Why don't you take your mother on a walk?"

My father, an introverted man who found it difficult to show or handle emotion, was relieved by this suggestion, and he and his mother set off together at once. Years afterward, my grandmother told me that this was the nicest thing my mother ever did for her.

FORTY-FIVE YEARS LATER, I'm an adult, married with children. We have just arrived in Machu Picchu and are climbing the sturdy stone stairs up from the rustic Sanctuary Lodge to the first vista point overlooking the abandoned city—a gray nest of organized boulders and stones perched high among the tops of the great green mountains, so tall that the white mist flows like the waters of a stream around their bases. Deliberately walking behind my father, I carefully match my pace to his laborious steps as the others spring ahead. *He's slowing down,* I think. The once tall, broad-shouldered man, full of strength and energy, is now, at eighty-seven, permanently hunched, shrunken, and fragile. Gray hair has replaced black; a whitening beard covers his once clean-shaven cheeks and the long, subtle dimples my older son has inherited.

He stops to take a breath at a landing between the giant stones that serve as stairs, leaning over and supporting himself with arthritis-mangled hands on freshly replaced knees. His sides heave quickly and the pale taupe of his safari vest, the vest with all the handy pockets for his wallet, glasses, and maps, rises and falls with his labored breathing. My eyes trace a bumpy line on his back, vertebrae pushing not only through his skinny frame but also through the material of his favorite travel outfit like the stones at Marin County's Pierce Point—large, lichen-covered boulders positioned in a straight line leading through the bluff, over the cliff, into the horizon.

Part of my father's strength is his stubbornness, and he's determined not to depend on others in his old age; he would rather die by his own hand than live helpless. In his sixties he bought *Final Exit,* a suicide how-to manual. Whenever I'm reminded of the line of stones at Pierce Point, I think of the romantic story that I now know is a myth: Long ago, the Miwok Indians placed the stones there as a sacred path to suicide, a death infused with symbols of infinite potential, cycles, and freedom. Invariably, like a record stuck in one groove, or a video frozen on one image, those stones and their fictional history make me think about my father—and I wonder now, as I wait with him on the steps of Machu Picchu, if he would still, twenty years later, attempt suicide if he felt he could no longer care for himself, if he sensed his independence slipping away, if he could no longer go on his beloved walks. But I'm too scared to ask outright the question I so blithely posed when I first spotted the book on the coffee table and he was only in middle age.

FOUR YEARS AFTER OUR TRIP to Machu Picchu, my father lies on the cracked sidewalk, already bleeding from the scrapes on his face and the palms of his hands. He has tripped in the dark and, not able to right himself, has fallen to the ground.

Over the next few days, his children confer. What is to be done? My father will not abandon his daily routine. For years we've given him blinking lights to secure to his belt, reflective patches for the back of his jacket, flashlights in all shapes and sizes, and even, once, a headlamp similar to those used by coal miners to light the pitch-black tunnels they must navigate. Nothing lasts with him.

Finally, because my father refuses to own a cell phone, my brother gives him a tracker, the better to monitor his movements. My father, ninety years old, still walks every day. Under Dutch elms, over driveways, past the Catholic church at the end of the first block. Sometimes it is dusk when he walks; often, night has already fallen. Neighbors know him from his limping gait, his plaid Pendleton shirt, his orthopedic shoes. They say they can hear him coming, as he periodically grunts and groans almost, but not quite, under his breath from the pain his bones and joints give him with every step. He sacrifices comfort for freedom, convenience for mobility.

PICTURE THIS: I'M WALKING IN the early morning, after school drop-off, before the errands and chores of the day begin in earnest. I walk briskly, hyperaware in my fifties of the benefits of raising my heart rate, moving my joints, and using my muscles. I also pause to take note of the heavy bunches of roses drooping over a fence, the moss that has grown over the decades on a stone bridge, as well as the rocks that form the creek bed underneath.

Sometimes I hike with a friend on trails through redwood groves, past views of mountains and valleys. We remark on our good fortune, we speak out loud our privilege: to be able to walk in such nature and spot, as if posing for a *National Geographic* spread, a blue heron or an osprey one day, ducks floating contentedly on the lake's calm surface or cormorants sunning themselves on a log the next.

One spring morning my friend and I sat on a wooden bench nestled in the bushes and trees mere feet from the water's edge. Chatting, conversing, gossiping, our faces angled toward the sun that filtered through the oak leaves and pine needles, we were visited by a baby otter. On its own, he—she?—seemed happy, not in the least lost or lonely. We sat as quietly as we could, whispering our delight with our visitor. She played around a bit at our feet, rolling in the shallow water, her glossy pelt gleaming darkly in the sun, sometimes submerging herself only to come back up a meter or two further on, either oblivious to our presence or wanting a kind of gentle communion with the two creatures sitting so still, so companionably, by the lake's shore.

Because I'm prone to the most sentimental type of nostalgia, I sometimes look back in time, even when immersed in the intense, often still startling beauty around me, and feel regret. I regret my immaturity in my youth, when I so thoughtlessly ignored my father, resentful of the forced daily marches through the neighborhood.

If I could go back with my experience and maturity now, to walk to the cow pond once again with my father, would I see more to appreciate? With the gratitude for physical beauty and familial bonding I've since learned, would I enjoy the pond walk more? Of course the answer is yes. But since I can't go back physically through a portal in time, can I at least rely on my memory to take me back forty or so years? Perhaps in this way I can see with fresh eyes what I took for granted when I felt too apathetic and lazy to go on a two-hour hike, and too resentful of my father for being such a mean, bossy dad who forced us to go on endless treks through dust and dirt and over canyons across flimsy log bridges with a pond full of defecating cows as the focal point. Maybe by relying on my memory and using my imagination, I can notice what I didn't care to notice on those original hikes. The sight and scent of the long row of tall eucalyptus decorating the top of the ridge with the white city of Quito on one side and a long, deep valley terraced in shades of green on the other. Our dogs, both adopted from the streets, trotting or running or smelling their way through the different tree trunks and bushes and grasses. The air, clean and pollution-free back then; the sky, either blue with white clouds or dark with impending rain; the hummingbirds, of which there were surely many kinds (Ecuador being famous for its variety of beautiful hummingbirds), flitting about here and there, all of them gleaming and shining, some sporting long, dramatic tailfeathers.

I regret, in my sentimentally nostalgic way, not appreciating these aspects of our walks as a child because I regret not being able to share this appreciation in real time, in the actual moment, with my father.

Today, though, I can make sure to collect photos that soothe me as screen savers of misty mornings on a reservoir, the dark tones of the evergreens muted by the softening white of the moist air, and of golden hills that reflect brightly, perfectly, on the still water of a lake. And, some weekends, I succeed in bribing my always-hungry sons with breakfasts of stacked pancakes, cheesy omelets, and thick French toast at a local diner in exchange for accompanying me on a hike.

It seems I've inherited my father's legacy after all.

Part Three

INNOCENCE LOST

Lima Golf

"ME FASTIDIA QUE HAY UNOS cholitos aquí en el golf. Mira esa mesa. Nos están choleando la comida." This comes from my aunt, complaining about another table of guests at the restaurant where we are eating our dishes of fresh fish, salad with avocado, and arroz con pollo.

Cholo: A derogatory South American term describing a mestizo, a person of mixed European and Amerindian descent, especially if the person is of low economic status.

It's 2019, and my mother and I have traveled together from our hometown in Northern California to Lima to visit family. We sit with my aunt, uncle, and cousin at their club in the middle of the city. This country club—surrounded first by lush rolling lawns closely cropped for golfers, then by a dense band of ferns, acacia trees, and bougainvillea, then, outside its high walls, by apartment buildings and penthouses—is highly exclusive. It isn't easy to belong, even if you have the money for the initial buy-in and the subsequent monthly dues. These days its exclusivity is predicated on legacy and old, established wealth.

We've come to the club to have a late lunch in the restaurant with sweeping views of the golf course. Waiters wear black-and-white uniforms, the tables are clothed in white linen, the walls are decorated with carefully curated Peruvian art. We always dress up to come to Lima Golf; it's a place where Limenean high society goes to see and be seen.

Choleaer: To make *cholo,* to render inferior, low-class.

I look in the direction of the table my aunt is talking about. But I already know what she refers to. I see what she sees. I noticed them before, these people sitting at that table, but I didn't articulate any thoughts consciously in my mind. Instead, I let this information lie dormant, drifting about, untended, until my aunt expressed her disfavor out loud.

At this same lunch the dark waiter has already put Splenda in my aunt's coffee, tearing open the packet he takes from its container on the table and shaking it with care into the cup he's just brought out for her. Another waiter, also dark, has buttered my younger cousin's bread for him.

The people seated at the table about whose presence my aunt is so outraged eat and converse ignorant, I hope, of the judgment emanating from her as we sit at our own table. They are shorter and darker than most of the other dining patrons; it is clear that they don't belong to the club. It looks to me like a business meeting. The customers at this table wear work-appropriate clothes, the women and men alike in some version of the business suit. It is the quality of the material, the finish of the cloth, the accessories, and even the haircuts that betray their class to the invested eye. And my aunt's eyes are definitely invested. She grew up in a world very strictly defined by class difference, by the educated, refined, white, and wealthy "haves" and the peasant or working-class, often uneducated, Indigenous or mestizo "have-nots." These innocent people eating in this exclusive club, possibly here for a company meeting with a CEO who is a member, are part of the growing middle class, but as such they are still offensive to my aunt.

There's a superiority of being, of self, so ingrained, so assumed, it's as if my family in Peru, especially my aunt, consider themselves a separate—and superior—species.

But there's a caveat to this story: I must say my aunt, as with most people on this earth, is not all bad. I love her, and I admire much about her too. There are other stories that seem to counteract or at least soften this automatic snobbery of hers.

She belongs to charity groups made up of rich, upper-class ladies who lunch. She's often in charge of collecting money and clothes for the orphanages. She also collects sad stories, and frequently recounts them to me—about impoverished and abused teenagers who kill themselves by jumping off the edge of the cliff in the very spot we are driving past; about sick babies left at church doorsteps by mothers unable to care for them; about a boy selling his wares on the street having his face slashed over a new pair of American sneakers he's managed to procure. She clucks and tsks as she talks, unhappy about the suffering around her.

When still a teenager, I once sat in the back of a car my aunt drove. I observed as she stopped and rolled down her window at the side of a dusty back road to scold a pair of dirty and barefoot kids, clearly siblings, who were yelling and clawing at each other in passionate disagreement. She ended her lecture about brotherly love with a clear order: *¡Tienen que quererse el uno al otro!*

Another story I have only heard about secondhand—but knowing my aunt, I can see her in my mind as if I were watching a video or hovering, specter-like, at the edges of the scene: My aunt drives her car again, confidently and capably steering the wheel and, I'm sure, chatting away to the passenger in the seat next to her (she's never alone; like my mother, she is a true extrovert and lonely when by herself). Then, once again, she stops her car. She has spotted a tableau that infuriates her. I didn't know before I heard this story that this kind of situation occurred in Peru; I had only heard of it in connection with India and the vast, established network there of human trafficking and begging. This is what my aunt sees, and this is what makes her press her foot on the brake, outraged: An abject group on a sidewalk. A mother and a father and at least one child. All of them poor, grimy, raggedy. The mother might have her hand out, mumbling blessings and entreaties in jumbled fragments, or it might be the father, his eyes pleading, face resigned. But it's not the child who begs. I know that for a fact, despite not having been there in person. Because the child, a little girl, is incapacitated, has been incapacitated. By her parents. On purpose. At the very least, they are drugging her for effect, or taking advantage of and prolonging a naturally occurring illness to display for philanthropic consumption. My aunt cannot bear this. She pulls to the side. She gets out and marches over to the family. Taking the child, she carries her back to the car and places her carefully on the back seat, all the while lecturing the parents angrily. She gets back into the car, slams the door shut, starts the engine, and drives off to take the little girl to the hospital, where she will pay for her emergency care.

A caveat to the caveat: This kind of justice that my aunt so passionately believes in and often acts on is the justice of the dominant class, the sense of fairness originating from the powerful. As *una patrona* she has the privilege to mete out her sense of justice in the same way she chooses to give out largesse. She acts as a kind of patron; she decides when and whom to give charity to—ideological charity, material charity, medical charity, absence-of-judgment charity. This social, political, economic, and even emotional terrain is no democracy, it is feudal.

Back at the restaurant, sitting with my relatives, enjoying the impeccable service, the beauty of the view outside, the comfort of the chairs, the delicious flavors of the lime- and avocado-infused food, my every wish the waiters' command, with the only crimp in my contentment being my aunt's contemptuous remarks about the table with the unsatisfactory clientele, I wonder if my mother notices what's unfolding before her—the classism that is exhibited so blithely, almost proudly, by her beloved sister. Or has she slipped back into her youthful upbringing, when she was taught every day with both word and example by her relatives, by her community, by her society, that darker Indigenous people are always and necessarily inferior to those who are lighter and whiter and richer?

I respond only by looking over at the table my aunt refers to, and listening to her. I react to her words and her contempt solely in my thoughts. Though I am outraged by her outrage that is so problematic to me in its unadulterated prejudice, I don't argue with her out loud. In the past, in the youth of my late teens and early twenties, I did try to bring up rights—those of women, those of the maids and the chauffeur and the gardeners, those, even, of animals—when visiting Peru. These attempted discussions fell on worse than deaf ears; they fell on ears suspicious and dismissive of conversational topics that seemed too earnest, too personal, too political, too negative. Every time until I finally gave up, I was made to feel—albeit subtly—a killjoy. I've reserved that kind of challenge my entire life mainly for my mother and father, both of whom were raised with their different prejudices around race and class. With them I've argued and shouted and gesticulated plenty of times; with them I've fought and I've cried. But with my aunt, who is also my godmother and almost always my hostess, I've learned to only watch and analyze.

I now see my aunt as a dinosaur of sorts. Some of her children and certainly her grandchildren don't hold the same racist values. What I want to believe is that my aunt's philosophy of life, her hierarchy of human citizenship that is based on skin color, on silk and cashmere over polyester and rayon, on club membership and trickle-down patronage, is on its way out.

Stalked

Tápame con tu rebozo, Llorona,
porque me muero de frío.

THIS STORY STARTS WITH HAIR, as mine often do.

When I was a sophomore in high school, my mother traveled to Peru for a family wedding. Without her I couldn't follow the maintenance routine I'd practiced religiously since puberty, when hormones contorted my relatively straight, well-behaved hair into a kinky mass of curl and frizz. Always with my mother's help, I performed the arduous process of occasional chemical straightenings and twice-weekly washings followed by hours under a home dryer.

During that same week, my best friend, a girl with stick-straight hair I envied, was asked to act as a model for an apprentice at Vidal Sassoon Salon. When another apprentice spotted me hovering, he offered to cut my hair for free as well. That moment signaled the end of my constant battles with my curls. I never straightened my hair the same way again.

My mother despaired when she returned home. Here was her oldest daughter, her ostensible mini-me, looking like *una salvaje*. For my mother, curly hair posed a direct and personal threat. She had it too, and had spent her own life controlling it with dryers and chemicals. Curly hair was wild, savage, unkempt, ugly—it was *deviant,* signifying brownness and blackness instead of the always coveted, the already superior smoothness of a certain kind of white women's hair she wanted for herself. But the damage was done. I refused to go back to the time-consuming, sometimes painful regimen she had bequeathed me as a matter of course.

Five years later, I sat on one of the black-and-chrome swivel chairs in a chic San Francisco salon. At some point after the stylist had begun his task of cutting my hair, he started a conversation with the client of the stylist next to us. To me she was magnificent-looking, as she probably was to many people. I learned from the conversation that she was married to a professional football player. In our culture, I'd already found out, rich football players who are big and handsome and blond do not marry awkward, frizzy-haired brown women; they marry resplendent blonde women, women with smooth, creamy skin, long, glossy hair, and shiny, polished nails. They marry beautiful white women who look like they were born expensively dressed, as this one was—her designer skirt and heels visible under her salon robe. While she talked, gold bracelets and a large diamond ring flashed with the movement of her hands. She was getting her hair highlighted in even brighter shades of blonde, and despite the silver foil decorating her head, I could tell that her hair was thick in a good way. The smooth locks I could see hanging over her shoulders positively shone in the light from a nearby window. She seemed to have a glow about her, a glow of beauty and privilege. She seemed to be a species alien to me.

I was soon entranced not only by her looks but by her conversation, by what she was recounting to my stylist and hers. Eavesdropping was easy—I'm sure she barely noticed me, sitting in my chair as my hair was being worked on, dark and quiet and shy, transfixed by her story.

"I walked into my house after my errand to put my bags down and when I turned around he was there . . . standing there, holding a gun."

There he stood, a man she didn't want in her life, who shouldn't have been a part of her life, yet someone known to her intimately: her stalker. This man had been following her for months and months—phoning, watching, writing, threatening. She had called 911, she had talked with the police, she had consulted with a lawyer, but they had all agreed: There was nothing they could do. The law forbade intervention until the stalker touched her, kidnapped her, raped her, or killed her.

"He wanted me to go back into the garage and get into the car with him, but then the phone rang. Thank God he let me answer, but he told me I had to pretend everything was normal."

It was her mother. At this point, this resplendent woman, this footballer's wife, had a brainstorm. To every straightforward question her innocent mother asked her, she gave a nonsensical answer.

"Did you remember to buy the hors d'oeuvres for tonight's party?"

"It was pretty crowded at the gym, yeah."

And so on. At one point her mother figured it out.

"Wait—is someone with you?"

"Yes, yes, I'll make sure to leave the package at your house."

"Is *that man* there?"

"Yes, of course, it won't be a problem."

"Oh my God, oh my God—don't worry, honey—I'm calling the police."

The football player's wife, we'll call her Cynthia, did her utmost to remain calm while trying every possible delaying tactic. She knew that getting into a car with this man to be taken to a second location meant certain death. Finally she could delay the transfer from house to car no longer, and she stepped from the lighted kitchen into the dark, closed garage, her stalker and his gun behind her.

As soon as they—stalker and obsession, man and woman, predator and prey—were both inside, lights flared, illuminating what once had been dark, what just a split second before had seemed a silent void. Men materialized, seemingly out of the woodwork—four, five, six men. Men with black uniforms, men heavily armed. Cynthia found out later that these highly trained agents had broken into the garage minutes prior, silently and stealthily, then hid themselves in the corners and among the shadows. The stalker didn't have a chance. He was grabbed, quickly and roughly, then handcuffed to be taken away. Cynthia, beautiful blonde Cynthia, had been rescued. She was safe.

Some time later I, a longtime devotee of Oprah Winfrey, watched this same resplendent woman, this poised football player's wife, tell her tale to the talk show host. She sat, majestic, next to Oprah on the stage, pantyhosed legs crossed and silky hair reflecting the studio lights like a halo. There had been a development in her story, a much-anticipated, long-worked-for development. Because of her near-death experience at the hands of her stalker, an event everyone knew was coming but nobody could intervene to stop, a new law had been put into place that offered women, at least on paper, protection from stalkers, peeping Toms, harassers, abusers, and would-be murderers *before* they touched their victims, abducted them, or inflicted physical harm. It seemed like a clear win for women, for feminists, for mothers who simply want to keep their daughters safe.

My husband and I watch a television series. It's historically based, all about drug cartels, government corruption, and death. We've entered a season partially set in the Mexican city of Juárez, with a subplot that involves a policeman approached by his neighbor, a mother who is worried about her missing daughter. Later he sees a young woman's mutilated body splayed on the ground, tape outlining the scene of the crime. At the morgue, carrying a photograph of the neighbor's daughter, he sees more dead bodies stacked up on makeshift shelves: all young, all female, all killed.

I know where this storyline is going. It refers to the hundreds of young women murdered in Juárez at the turn of the century. I remember reading about it in graduate school, the "femicide" of the young maquiladora workers. What I recall in particular was the mystery surrounding the murders. Newspapers and magazines claimed that no one knew exactly when or where or why these female factory workers were being killed. There were no arrests or even dedicated investigations; there was no national outcry or international concern. None, at least, that was sustained and effective.

My husband looks up the murders on his phone for me. He wonders what to type into the search engine. "Hundreds of young women murdered in Juárez?" I suggest.

"Juárez or Mexico?"

"Juárez!" I repeat. "Juárez! It was a *thing*. And it was mostly factory workers. All in *Juárez*." I'm pretty impassioned at this point, and impatient—I can't see why he doesn't understand that it was a huge deal at the time, at least to me, and horrific, the reality of hundreds of young women murdered, all the same in terms of class and race and age and look, with no answers for their mothers and fathers, brothers and sisters. Just disappearance. Then, maybe, a body. Only a body.

He finds out there is *still* no answer for the murders, for the uniformity and number of the victims. And that the killings continue today, over two decades later. No one seems to care. The world goes on, the implicit message being it's just women, *muchachas*, maquiladora workers. Just brown women. Just poor women.

The photos included in the articles I remember from years ago featured young women with black or brown hair. Mostly long. Usually thick. Dark hair in simple ponytails or braids. Unhighlighted, uncolored, unmaintained. In the television series as well, the young workers file out of the factories and into the buses waiting for them, walking and talking, all with dark skin, all with dark hair—shades of black, shades of brown.

A FEW YEARS AGO, I WATCHED a film about the unsolved murders and disappearances of Indigenous women across Canada and the United States, in cities and towns and reservations. Although set in Wyoming and filmed in Utah, the movie speaks to the over four thousand (and still counting) Native girls and women missing or murdered in the last thirty years, over one hundred a year, at least three a week. What would happen, asks the movie's subtext, if white women were stolen at this rate?

Because it's Hollywood, the plot is driven by a white male savior and his white female sidekick. Both have fair skin, lighter hair. The central crime of the narrative involves a young woman who dies, barefoot in the middle of a winter night, while running from her predator. The image that has stayed in my head all these years is her hair, thick and black and long, spread over the sparkling white snow.

SINCE 2016 AND BEFORE the pandemic, I've participated in several of the annual Women's Marches in San Francisco. At one of these, I stood listening to the speakers at the rally, before the actual walk from the Civic Center down Market Street to the Embarcadero near the Ferry Building. A Native American speaker was remembering the women missing or murdered in the past year. Some women on the platform alongside her carried posters with the names and faces of those taken, all of whom had brown skin, black hair. I noticed that the women on the platform, as well as many milling close around it, also had dark hair, hair like mine. Thick and coarse, long and wavy, black or brown.

The woman at the microphone exhorted us to say their names out loud. "Say their names!" she called to us. "Say their names!" Then, one by one, as if lines in a poem, she pronounced the names of more than thirty women: Indigenous, Black, Latina.

Solemnly, respectfully, the crowd chanted them back at her, my voice rising to join theirs. Yet today I cannot recall a single name. Only that all of the women, all of those missing and murdered, had dark hair.

MY MOTHER PROBABLY SAID "*Ten cuidado*" many times when I was growing up as I left the house to drive somewhere, to go to school, to go to a party, to fly to another state or country. She still says it, or something like it, every time we say goodbye on the phone. Variations on the theme of awareness and precaution: *Don't forget about . . . Remember to . . . Be sure to . . . Drive carefully . . . Watch out for . . . Close the windows . . . Lock the door . . . Be careful . . . Take care.* My mother is a classic helicopter parent, the Latina mother, the South American *mamá*. She is always thinking about her children, the dangers threatening them at all times, especially her two daughters—harassment, mugging, assault, kidnapping, rape, murder. If I had to guess (direct questioning feeling too complicated and awkward), I would say that these fears, the conscious fears of physical threat to her daughters, are because we are daughters not sons, because we are female rather than male. I don't think that my mother is consciously afraid of the dangers that may threaten us because we are Latinas, because we have inherited her curly hair, because I, at least, have inherited her darker skin.

When I was growing up, my mother constantly nagged me to straighten my hair, to sport the look and style of the Anglo blondes who had smooth, silky locks. She wanted me to "take care" of myself—wear my retainers, shave under my arms, straighten my hair. As a teenager, I could bring her to the verge of tears with my defiant defense of my frizzy, unkempt hair. Yet she didn't have that same fervor when facing my sister's curls—and I think that was because my sister was the fairest of all my mother's children. Instead of straightening, my mother's dream for my sister's hair was highlighting. She loved it when a summer in the sun bleached my sister's brown hair shades of gold, or when my sister experimented with blonde highlights at the salon.

My sister does easily what I can sometimes achieve: pass. She always passes as white, not only in other countries and cultures where the greater population is darker-skinned than her but also anywhere in the United States or Europe. Her fair skin that burns easily, her lighter hair, and her soft brown eyes all say white, not brown or Black or mixed or Other. I, on the other hand, have the kind of look that says, although ambiguously, *not* white. But a question remains: If not white, then what? I have been mistaken, especially when younger and tanner and bigger-haired, for light Black, for Black and white, for Greek or Arab, for Lebanese or Brazilian.

When I was eleven, my family went on a jungle cruise down Ecuador's Napo River. One morning before heading out on canoes to the island where the howler monkeys lived, I watched as our father carefully smoothed sunscreen on the faces of my sister and brother before applying it to his own. Curious as to why I was being left out of this fastidious ritual, I asked my father why he wasn't putting sunscreen on my face. "Because you don't need it," he told me. "You don't burn like your brother and sister." At that moment my family was segregated along color lines: my father and siblings on the fragile white side, my mother and I on the resilient brown side.

Yet I never felt from my mother—or my father, come to think of it—conscious fear for me as potential prey because of my black hair or my darker skin. Instead, with the benefit of experience and hindsight, I think now that my mother's *Ten cuidado*, repeated over time and in various iterations, came from a sublimated fear. An unexamined knowledge, almost instinctual, that smooth, straight hair meant *mainstream*, which, in turn, could mean more options and greater safety. Much of her maneuvering for my sister to have blonder hair and for me to have straighter hair seems to have had an unconscious goal: whiteness.

IMAGINE A WOMAN, A DARK woman, a woman with brown skin, black hair. This woman lives in the Canal District of my home county in Northern California, a neighborhood on the "other side of the tracks," a neighborhood populated almost exclusively by Latinos, many of whom are immigrants, some of whom are undocumented. This woman lives in an apartment building, in a unit she shares with ten others, an extended family. She does not have a famous football player husband; she does not have a garage. What this woman does have: a stalker. Does she go to the police? No, she does not. The police may arrest her; they may deport her—she knows at the very least they will ignore her. What she also does not have: recourse. So her stalker stalks her. He continues to spy and harass and monitor and threaten. Finally the day comes when someone calls the police for her. But it is too late. She is another dark-skinned body, another black-haired corpse.

"Take care," they say, the dark-haired mothers and sisters and aunties and grandmothers, the dark-haired coworkers and colleagues and friends. "Take care." From studies and interviews we know that across Mexico and Canada and the United States, "take care" has become almost a mantra, a prayer, a spoken amulet given to young dark-haired women before they leave home or school or the office or a party. What is a common, almost meaningless expression to many has become a supplication to the gods. Without options or resources, without recourse, they create a magic spell, an incantation, one they use and reuse, hoping ever faithfully even when the words become worn and faded, even when they know words don't work.

The Snack Vendor

My mother's snobbery was a many-splendored thing. At least it was so when I was growing up and most responsive to her influence. Or perhaps, because snobbery is such a negative quality, I should say instead that my mother's was many-armed: Like a colonizing octopus with continuously seeking tentacles, it popped up at seemingly random moments, not necessarily restricted to earnest lectures at home about starting my period or using bad words.

One such instance of my mother's particular brand of snobbery has stayed in my mind, an embarrassing incident, painful proof to me of my youth and naïveté: In my middle school years, when we lived in Ecuador, we belonged to a country club consisting of a pool, locker rooms, a sprinkling of patio tables and lounge chairs, and a snack shack. Although I was shy, at thirteen I was beginning to test the possibilities of my persona: the potential of an outgoing, talkative self. I was exploring my power to charm not only as an adult but as a woman. Perched on a round barstool at the counter in the snack shack, I swiveled gently to and fro, back and forth, clad only in a bikini, my hair wet, my body still long and angular and mostly flat-chested, chatting, exchanging questions, possibly flirting (if so, oh how mildly, how cautiously) with the man stationed behind the counter to take orders and prepare food.

How old was this employee? I can't tell even now, forty-plus years later. He might have been twenty-five, thirty. But more importantly, more crucially for my mother than his age and sex, was his class.

When it came to class, my Peruvian mother was so strict she assumed obvious and insurmountable boundaries between me and the man behind the counter. The counter, to her, signified a wall of some weighty kind, a class barrier made tangible. Because I was barely thirteen years old, to me the barriers to overcome were between child and adult, male and female, play and flirtation. I felt the thrill of exploring the boundaries I knew were meant to be pushed, at least eventually. I felt a rush of power, unfamiliar to me and yet instantly recognizable as belonging to the age-old, millennia-honed arena of instinct.

But to my mother, brought up in a culture of implacable class hierarchies, I was behaving inappropriately, and my banter, my talk, my use of his first name, was wrong and embarrassing, a major faux pas. She lectured me about it later, saying I shouldn't socialize with the poolside snack vendor, who was, after all, not only "the help" but also a man more Indigenous than European in skin tone and facial features.

When I protested—"Why not? What's the big deal?" And, finally, "Is it because you think he's not as good as us?"—she replied in the affirmative. *Sí.* We were better than him, superior: Our wealth, our education, our way of speaking, our houses and clothes and cars proved it so. Not, as she would readily admit if I pressed her, in a spiritual way, not in the next life, not before the eyes of God. But in this life, in this secular world, boundaries and barriers had to be erected, lines not only drawn in the sand but also carved in stone so that civilized people, *refined* people, *la gente fina,* would not have to mix with *la gente chola.* Unsaid by her—unthought by her, I'm sure—was that such sociopolitical barriers between the upper and the lower classes were necessary to maintain the power and privilege of people like us, born into wealth and affluence because of the complicated history of conquest and colonialism, of race and ethnicity and exploitation.

I know about that history now, as an adult, as an academic, as an observer whose heart hurts at the sight of a grubby little girl alone in some dingy corner or a father begging on the street for *limosna* to buy food for his children. I know how my mother was carefully educated in this history's various precepts, in its complex and entrenched forms of racial and class prejudice. She grew up thinking it normal to have a maid prepare your breakfast and, while you ate it, make your bed and tidy your room before returning to clear your mess on the table. She watched without judgment as her sister looked through the maids' handbags on their way out of the house on their single day off a week for stolen goods—jewelry or silver or *soles*. Her voice broke with righteous emotion when she reprimanded a maid during a stay at my aunt's house for shoving my little cousin; she was outraged, saddened, indignant, never thinking of the constant drip, drip, drip of abuse that this little bratty cousin of mine, her spoiled, rude niece, inflicted on the young, often teenage maids. (I remember this particular incident because I felt the injustice of the young maid, with her round brown face and long black braid, being disciplined while my cousin, the initial perpetrator, the instigator, stood smugly in front of her visiting aunt, further defended by the protective hands my mother placed on her shoulders.)

My mother stopped having a maid come to our own house when we lived in Ecuador because it annoyed her that, to her eyes, this maid took advantage by bringing her baby to work and washing her waist-length hair in the unused servant quarters before she left in the evening. Later, she would call the police of our small affluent California town to complain of the immigrant laborers hanging about the corners looking for day work. Her world, that of the forties and fifties and sixties in Peru, was not one of contextualization, of recognizing the systemic power inequities that created and maintained class difference and the boundaries that were deemed not only necessary but also natural, normal, always and already in place.

That day at the swim club, when she admonished me for being too friendly with the snack vendor, my mother asked, *"¿Te puedes imaginar a tu prima Carlita actuando así? ¿Hablando como amigos con un mozo?"* She wanted to know if I could possibly imagine, in my wildest dreams, my first cousin Carlita, the eldest daughter of my aunt Carla, talking in such a friendly manner to a common waiter. Carlita represented the highest standard of feminine behavior in my mother's family. She was beautiful in a quiet way, and almost painfully elegant in her affect. She had graduated from a Swiss finishing school, the type that hosts European royalty and American millionaires, as well as Middle Eastern princes and princesses. She was continuously held up to me by my mother as a role model, as a living template of ideal femininity to which to aspire as I chose my words, my mannerisms, my hairstyle, my clothes, even—or especially—my friends.

ALTHOUGH IT'S TRUE THAT MY mother's snobbery, sometimes an automatic reflex, sometimes a conscious expression, reigns supreme in many of the scenes of my past, it is also true that she is capable of beautiful and often spontaneous compassion. Children in particular pull at her heart, compelling her to act. For years my mother sent twenty US dollars every month to Lima for the education of a young boy after she learned he'd had to stop attending middle school in order to help his family make money to live on. These depended-on twenty dollars, reliably delivered, were enough to enable him to finish his schooling and attend a community college, thus educating himself to enter a profession rather than the manual labor that unrelenting poverty would otherwise have forced upon him.

My grandmother had a maid who'd been with the family for most of her life. Jesusa was a young teenager when she left her Andean home to work for "las Tías," the three spinster aunts who lived together in a crucifixed and rosaried house in Miraflores, a pleasant residential neighborhood in Lima. Jesusa entered this home as a young girl and only left after all three of the spinster sisters died. She left that home, which las Tías donated to the Catholic Church in their joint will, to live and work at my grandmother's house a few blocks away. After my grandmother died at 103, my mother, wanting to reward Jesusa for her dedicated service to her mother and aunts, gave her thirty thousand dollars to buy a small house in a middle-class neighborhood. This gift enabled Jesusa to become a landlady, further allowing her, in turn, to do the unthinkable for a poor uneducated maid, the daughter of peasants, a person descended from the mountains: class up.

Even here, in the United States, in our wealthy Northern California county where there typically aren't darker, poorer people sitting in the dirt waiting with hands out for assistance, my mother found ways to help. Driving one day in the business section of a nearby town, passing grocery stores and gas stations, she saw a young Latina woman step down from a bus, juggling her purse and shopping bags as well as her plump, smiley baby. She watched at a stoplight as this overburdened mother struggled to walk down the street toward her destination, wherever that might have been.

When the light turned green, my mother made a sudden, sharp U-turn and retraced her route until she arrived outside the local children's store. There she found a sturdy stroller, which she paid for and stored in her trunk. Then, getting back in the car, she drove around for several minutes, passing the car dealerships and auto mechanics, until she spotted the young mother and her cute baby once again and was able to stop and offer the stroller. Her companion on these errands that day told me about the surprise and relief in the young woman's face when she realized she was being given this stroller that would carry her baby as well as her purse and bags.

THERE IS ANOTHER STORY, THOUGH—one that always accompanies these scenes in my mind, one that is not so pleasant, not so positive. It's not a terrible story, not a violent one with blood or bruising, or even cutting words. Instead it is an ordinary story of mundane, normalized cruelty.

On a visit to Peru, my sister and I accompany my grandmother and older cousin on errands. My cousin Carlita, she of immaculate femininity and careful sophistication, drives. As always, she looks elegant, her hair back in a sleek ponytail, a delicate gold chain around her tan neck, manicured nails gleaming with polish at the end of long, thin fingers.

She leaves the car to do some quick shopping in a local strip mall near the gated community where my aunt and uncle live. My grandmother and sister and I elect to wait in the car.

It's hot, and the nearby acacia tree dripping with pods isn't close enough to provide shade. The car in which we sit is old, and there's no air conditioner to cool us if we leave the engine on. So we sit in the heat, windows mostly down, the air inside and out heavy and warm. We are in my grandmother's white Volkswagen, the car she's had my entire life. My grandmother loves this car—the one she purchased when widowed at forty-eight, the one that has given her independence in the second half of her life—and often talks about it with affection, as if it were a cherished pet or family member.

As we sit in this car, a band of poor boys approaches my grandmother's window. They crowd around, clamoring to clean the windows for some *propina*. My grandmother accepts with a nod of her silver-bunned head. A couple of boys swipe and wipe with their rags, one on each side of the windshield. My grandmother demands a more thorough job. Soon there is only one boy who continues his attempts to please the rich old lady in the white car, the señora with pearls around her neck and diamonds on her fingers. Unfortunately, he is a small boy and has to jump to reach the top of the glass. My grandmother is merciless. He must complete the job properly or he won't get any money from her. Gamely, he jumps and jumps, his short arms reaching up as he swipes his rag desperately at the flecks of dust my grandmother points out to him from inside with a dictatorial finger.

My sister cannot take this any longer. She is furious on behalf of the raggedy little boy who is not big enough to reach the entire windshield. From her seat next to me in the back, she calls out to our grandmother in angry Spanish.

For the life of me, I can't recall today what my sister said to our grandmother. Of course she did not say, "*Eres una racista*." That wasn't in our shared vocabulary with our relatives in Peru, especially with our grandmother, who was born in 1908 and raised in Lima's rigid class system. But she probably said, in Spanish, something like, "Stop that! Don't you see he can't reach? Give him money *now*—you're being totally unfair!"

After her explosion, my sister gets out of the car in a huff, slamming the door behind her. The Volkswagen my grandmother has treasured for decades shakes in the wake of her departure.

I don't remember what my grandmother said at that point, or if she said anything at all. If she didn't assume that my sister was being moody and instead realized that something was wrong, she would have done so only vaguely, confusedly. Certainly she would not have understood that she was being condemned for her racism, for the entitled elitism she took for granted as her right.

THERE IS YET ANOTHER STORY, this one associated forever with the story of the beggar boy and our dictatorial grandmother—because, again, of my sister's reaction. But this time I am the object of her outrage. Did I deserve the same censure as my grandmother? You be the judge.

On another visit to Lima, my family—aunt and uncle, mother and siblings, a few cousins—are driving in two, probably three, cars to a famous restaurant on a cliff overlooking the sea. I am thirsty. So incredibly thirsty. My head throbs. As I look out the window, I see the ubiquitous signs and billboards for Coca-Cola and start fantasizing about a large, cold glass of Coke that I drink in gulps without stopping.

Whatever I drink in Peru, whether water or soda or juice, has to be bottled, because tap water is dangerous for "gringos" like me. My stomach, unlike my mother's, is not immune to the bugs in the water, and if I'm not careful I'll be bedridden with nausea and vomiting.

I want to stop and buy a soda from one of the many kiosks on the street, but everyone in my car votes to continue to the restaurant, reluctant to make us late for the others. So instead I sit in the back seat, willing the car to go faster, to get to the restaurant quickly, so that I can order a Coke and end my malaise—the fatigue, the headache, the thirst. My fantasy evolves and now I drink and drink from a glass of cold Coke and then jump into a deep blue lake, covering myself with cool, clean water, absorbing hydration through every pore.

When at last we arrive at the restaurant and walk through the lobby, we pass a low bench. It's all I can do to stop myself from lying down and resting my head.

After the host seats us at a long table alongside the window facing the sea, a waiter approaches to ask for our orders, pad of paper in hand. He, like all the waiters in Lima, is brown. I ask for *"una Coca-Cola, por favor . . . sin hielo."* I repeat: *"Sin hielo."* By then I'd learned the hard way that ice in Lima is not made with boiled or bottled water. Like a Trojan horse, it looks innocent but contains the microorganisms that can temporarily destroy good health and well-being. Then I wait, pulsing with impatience, trying not to give in to the urge to lay my head on the table. Where is that Coke? I can't concentrate on the menu, cannot follow the conversations around me. My whole being focuses, laser-sharp, on drinking a Coca-Cola.

Finally I see the waiter approaching with a tray of drinks. But when he places my glass on the table in front of me, I see that it has ice in it. I close my eyes. I can't believe it. *"Dije 'sin hielo.' Pedí una Coca-Cola ¡sin hielo!"* I am not gentle; I am not patient.

The waiter apologizes and takes away the glass with the offensive ice. After a few minutes I finally get my Coke without ice, and I feel better as soon as I drink it. But my sister is angry. She is incensed at my behavior. How dare I treat the waiter that way? I was rude, I was insulting, I yelled at him. And finally, the coup de grâce, *"You're such a racist!"*

Now *I'm* angry.

"I wasn't being racist," I say. "I was desperate for a drink. And I asked him specifically for no ice!"

"Would you act that way with a waiter in the States?" she demands.

"Of course!" I insist. "If someone gets a specific order wrong and brings me the *opposite* of what I asked for, then it doesn't matter where we are; obviously, I'd get upset."

My sister doesn't believe me.

Long after the conversation is over, I continue to smart from her accusation. I defend myself in my head. I was dehydrated, intensely so, and also ironically—because the reason for my dehydration was my phobia of accidently drinking tap water and getting sick, I had been avoiding drinking altogether, at least subconsciously. My frustration with the waiter, then, was not personal, or raced, or classed. I may have been disrespectful, but the rudeness was triggered by my headache and malaise, not by his skin color or facial features.

HERE IN NORTHERN CALIFORNIA, in the county across the Golden Gate Bridge that I call my home, I had a gardener for a while who was brown. His name was Juan, and I called him "Don Juan" when I talked about him as my mother did, but I avoided calling him anything in face-to-face conversations because I was unsure about the protocol in this country. There was an awkwardness between us—mostly on my side, but a little on his too.

If we had been employer and employee in South America—in Peru or Ecuador, for example—there would have been no awkwardness. We would both have known how to address each other, what the parameters of our relationship were. Here, though, things are constantly in flux, and culture continuously changes and evolves. Although brown people in my county, the "Hispanics" and the "Latinos," are mostly segregated in their own "wrong side of the tracks," we both knew, Don Juan and I, that we were in a different kind of place here, that we were at least supposed to be living in a democracy, that we believed, collectively, as a nation, in equality regardless of class or race. So we interacted in a kind of limbo, that uncomfortable, in-between space where I knew the rules of the two cultures informing our behavior but didn't know which ones were most appropriate to use in our different, blended circumstances. We would chat about our families—mostly his, as I was in some ways still "La Patrona." But he would call me by my first name in texts about the yard, while other gardeners I've had, also originally from Central or South America, always called me simply "Señora." He had less of the deference in speech, tone, and body language that domestic workers in Central and South America more recently arrived in the United States have toward their employers. He problem-solved with me about the garden as an equal. He offered to take care of things like pest control and tree trimming instead of outsourcing them.

Things were going along swimmingly, and the awkwardness I'd felt at the beginning was no longer there. Until the ask.

DON JUAN INVITES ME TO his youngest child's christening party. This is code, I believe, for becoming a godparent. Not in the formal religious way, dressed up and standing with the family at the baptismal font as a priest sprinkles holy water on the infant's forehead, but in an informal, primarily financial way. My aunt in Lima is the "godmother" of several maids' children. She can be counted on to give presents and money on birthdays and special occasions. I sense that this is what Don Juan wants from me. Of course, I could be wrong, but my instincts tell me it is so. I don't mind buying a one-time present, but what gives me trouble is not only the responsibility of becoming a lifelong patron but also, more immediately, of attending the party in person. That may have been Don Juan's riff on the new system—the better system, the more democratic system.

In Lima or Quito, the *madrinas* chosen from the employer class don't go to the actual parties in the dusty villages surrounding the city. They dispense largesse, usually in the form of cash, from their gated community mansions, their luxury high-rise apartments, or their lush colonial estates. Perhaps Don Juan thought of me as both a moneyed godmother to his child *and* a regular friend who could join quite naturally in the christening festivities, eating rice and grilled meat, chatting in Spanish and English and Spanglish, listening to Latin pop and reggaeton.

Whatever Don Juan's actual thoughts, I know my own reaction: Every social instinct I've internalized over the years—living in Ecuador and the Philippines, visiting Peru, listening to my mother's admonitions and lectures, watching her and my aunt and my grandmother interact with maids and gardeners—protests at the thought of accepting this invitation. I imagine myself going to the party in a neighborhood so different from mine in a European car, wearing designer clothes, with diamond studs in my ears and gold rings on my fingers. I could, I also realize, wear a more basic outfit, eschew jewelry, park a block down the street. Yet still there's something off about the idea of walking into this house carrying my wrapped present, greeting Don Juan, being introduced to his wife and children and friends, finding a place to sit or stand, making small talk . . . with whom? What would I say after comments about the food and questions about children? I fear being overwhelmed by the awkwardness built into *mutual* lifetimes of class acculturation, the unspoken yet keenly felt differences in education, intellectual interests, conversational subjects. What would the other guests think of me, a sore thumb sticking out among them? My socialization has warped my visceral reactions to the point where trying to align my values and behavior in this situation gives me paralyzing anxiety. What am I to do?

I call my sister. Although we've never spoken about her past accusation, the one of naked racism toward the distracted brown waiter at the seaside restaurant in Lima, I trust her now, decades later, to be able to advise me; she is one of the only people in the world who knows intimately the nuances of our family history and cultural identity.

She gets what I'm saying right away. In only a few sentences, she grasps the entirety of my conundrum. Her advice: Don't go to the party. Make an excuse for why I can't attend. But buy a gift for the baby to present to Don Juan on one of his gardening days at my house.

I take only part of her advice—the part that agrees with my problematic instincts. I don't go to the party. I can't help thinking that he might not be expecting me to actually show up, that he might be using this ask not as an actual invitation to attend the party in person but to elect me as an informal madrina. But in this in-between space that is the United States and its culture of denied and glossed-over classism and racism, I cannot find out directly; I can only stumble about in the dark, hands outstretched, trying to move forward without falling.

I'm ashamed to admit that neither do I decide on an appropriate gift—a needed one perhaps, one that would be appreciated—and then purchase it and prepare it with care in order to present it to Don Juan as a token of my investment in the well-being of his family and the future of his children. The conundrum—the accumulated life lessons from my upbringing, the question as to whether or not I should accept the invitation, the guilt about possibly refusing the invitation—becomes so overwhelming, I ignore it until it's too late. The day of the party passes and the celebrations occur without the godmother, without even a gift.

Although this situation occurred a few years ago, I still feel guilty. But it is a muted guilt. I can't force a happy ending, a neat tying-up of loose ends, the smug knowledge of a lesson learned as if a box checked. Since my initiation into my mother's worldview that day when she spotted me talking to the snack vendor, I've been continuously schooled by my mother's admonitions as to how I should and shouldn't behave. She may not have meant to, as she is a kind and gentle mother, but she shamed me into seeing the world in a certain way: through the lens of class prejudice. Once baptized into a closed community by a mother loved completely and unreservedly, how to purge oneself later in life of the values so repeatedly internalized since?

To be a madrina means to sponsor a baby at baptism, but godmotherhood can mean so much more: making sure the child grows up to be a good Catholic, or favoring the child with time and money and gifts, or, in its most extreme form, adopting the godchild if its parents die. When Don Juan asked me to attend the christening party of his child, he may have been asking me to become an informal madrina. Yet this ask had for me a huge subtext, an underground warren of assimilated values and learned reactions, of visceral reflexes that warred constantly with the precepts of a belief system I had begun to embrace intellectually in college.

How do we de-baptize ourselves? How do we reverse the process of initiation? It can happen with initiation into a counter-discourse, with baptism into a new community of thought. That's what happened to me. I was baptized anew again and again in college and graduate school, baptized by scholar-priests as if by fire: W. E. B. Du Bois, Zora Neale Hurston, James Baldwin, Rigoberta Menchú, Ana Castillo, Frantz Fanon, Sandra Cisneros, Edward Said, Gloria Anzaldúa, Toni Morrison . . . The list goes on. These baptisms purged as they burned, the licking flames cleansing my mind of the corrupt and the fetid. Yet—not quite. Because dealing with the mind, it turned out, was not enough. I have in my body and in my psyche, as if by muscle memory, these early internalized, value-laden reactions to life—to experiences, situations, scenarios, to the negotiation of options and choices, to the making of decisions. I may have thought myself free of the prejudices my mother inculcated in me since birth through advice and remonstrance and modeling, yet Don Juan and the passive decisions I made through procrastination show me I am not. I may have come a long way from my mother's initial stance toward those darker or poorer than us, as she has done herself, but I have not divorced myself from those values in a tidy or clean way.

What is baptism, after all? As ritual, it symbolizes purification and regeneration. I was baptized by shame rather than water when my mother sought to purify me of what she saw as corrupting: the casual interaction with the snack vendor, a man of a different caste—poorer, browner, less educated. Some Christians only baptize after the onset of the age of reason. When a person has reached a level of self-awareness. When a person can *choose*. This was the case with many of my friends at the missionary school in Quito. Instead of the sprinkling of holy water on an infant's head, there was total submersion in pools at the ages of eleven, twelve, maybe thirteen. When I was baptized as a baby in a Catholic church, I obviously had no awareness, no thought, no choice. My aunt is my madrina. She rarely speaks of church and I've never seen her go to Mass; the values she preaches and models are the social and the material. She is like my mother on steroids when it comes to image consciousness, to worshipping money and all it can bring: gated-community estates, deluxe apartments, chauffeured cars, gold and silver and diamonds and pearls, designer clothes, beach condos, country club memberships.

It is separate from my mother's class consciousness, away from my aunt's status worship, that I chose to be baptized, to be born over and over again into communities I found in classrooms in Berkeley and Seattle, in the pages of *A People's History of the United States*, *Playing in the Dark*, *This Bridge Called My Back*, and *I Know Why the Caged Bird Sings*, and in journals like *Bitch* and *The Sun*.

Once, only a decade or so ago, I came home to find my mother waiting for me. She'd picked up a magazine lying in the pile of mail on my kitchen counter and perused its contents—to her horror. The magazine, *Adbusters*, spelled out in black and white and every color in between—the red of blood, the orange of danger, the blue of bruising—the atrocities of imperialism, colonization, capitalism, militarism, dictatorship, and patriarchy . . . what had become for me the usual suspects. She found images, photographs, words and phrases and sentences, all brutal in their truth-telling. Each picture, each article exposed the seamy, sordid, exploitive underbellies of our world. Although I don't remember the exact contents of that edition, it could easily have contained an exposé of our animal agriculture that tortures animals while destroying our environment, or pictures of sweatshops here and abroad where women and often children are locked into airless factories overnight to finish a job, or the truths of sex trafficking both in the United States and around the world.

My mother waved the magazine at me accusingly, her voice breaking with emotion as she asked, *"¿Qué es esto?"* She demanded an explanation. She wanted to know why I had such a thing in my possession. *"¡No debes tener una revista como esta en la casa!"* To her, the magazine was itself an atrocity; it was so hideous, so ugly and awful that it scared her. What to me was a cleansing baptism by fire was to her an immersion in a dangerous cesspool of depravity.

I defended my magazine by first accusing her of snooping and then claiming my right to have anything I wanted in my house—but I was shaken. Her outrage and her tears made me feel bad for her and depressed for myself because they reminded me of the widening schism between my values and hers—how what I could read with admiration and curiosity was something akin to the devil's handbook in my mother's eyes.

I don't like remembering the moment in my kitchen with my mother and the charged text she begged me to throw away. I feel sad for both of us, mostly for my mother, and embarrassed for both of us, mostly for me. Yet just last week I had a friend over, and she talked about her recent trip to Lima to visit long-estranged family. Her uncle and his children confessed they'd been worried about what to wear to their first meeting, and she remarked to me how "class consciousness" is still a strong cultural phenomenon in Peru. We also talked, in a non-related manner, about gardens, and how I had always, until only a few years ago, unthinkingly assumed that plants—trees and shrubs and flowers—were permanent. That once planted they just grew until adulthood, then stayed the same. I knew they changed seasonally but never thought consciously that they actually died, that they had a distinct and, some of them, not-too-long lifespan and thus needed replacement. But of course they do die, and many have under my watch in the last twenty years we've lived in our home.

These two parts of the same conversation, not related in any obvious way, connected in my mind. How class consciousness can be a massive force, like a sneaker wave—a tsunami, even. How people, especially children, can be swept away by its precepts, its rules, its attitudes toward people and their roles in society. It also brought to my mind the idea of a garden, of plants and their upkeep. The idea of pruning. That Don Juan and I, both on our sides, were like gardeners pruning a tree, a tree that is our distinct selves and our relationship, how we were constantly snipping here and there to improve this tree so that it could grow and flourish. Pruning away the dead bits, the rotten and corrupt leaves and twigs, in order to allow for a fresh cycle.

TODAY I MET WITH SAMUÉL, our latest gardener. He's originally from Mexico, and though he does speak rudimentary English, I usually speak Spanish with him.

It's been a full six years since the christening invitation conundrum with Don Juan and its guilt-ridden aftermath.

I don't call our current gardener "Don Samuél," as I might have if my mother were still alive, as I once called Juan "Don Juan," and her Guatemalan gardener "Don Roberto," and our handyman from decades ago in Ecuador "Don José." Instead I call him simply Samuél.

When we met today we both stood on the patio, discussing mudslides, broken pipes, irrigation, and riprap. At one point I sat at the wrought iron table to write a list of issues to talk over later with my husband. I noticed after a minute of listening, questioning, and transcribing that Samuél was standing in the sun, sweating in the heat. It was mid-August, and the temperature in the mid-eighties. The sun beat down on the patio, and yet Samuél remained standing. I think he did so because he is an employee, or perhaps because he is a gardener and standing outdoors is part of his persona, but it could also be because we inhabit that same in-between social space, that cultural limbo of transitional behavior norms, *la frontera* between the rigid classification of racialized bodies in strict, ladderlike hierarchies and the purported democracy of the northern Americas where regardless of types of labor—manual or technical or intellectual—everyone is supposed to be equal, of equal worth, equally human.

I asked him to sit at the table with me, if he would like to, and get out of the sun underneath the patio umbrella. "*Siéntate,*" I said, "*está muy caliente en el sol.*"

Even as I uttered these words and watched him take a seat, my mind harked back to Don Juan. Was I enacting a kind of penance? With my words? With my ask? Yes, I like to think. And more than penance, a naturalization—a normalization—of a truly democratic way of being.

Death Tax

What's happening?

I'm in the bed I share with my husband. Only three weeks have passed since my mother died. It's midnight or the early hours of the morning; it could also be soon after I fall asleep. And this is definitely a falling, not a drifting. I've fallen and, like the old lady, I'm trying to get up but can't. I'm trying to get up and out of somewhere dark and disorienting, for this is no refreshing pool of water on which to float, or quiet, calm room in which to meditate. I've fallen into an abyss.

I can't see!

The darkness crushes me, stifling—a pillow pressed against my face. The darkness bears down on me, too close. I am scrabbling, flailing. This darkness—a bully. Relentless.

Where am I?

But what I really mean is, *Where are you?*

When I'm on my computer, taking a break from emails or writing, I watch the photos appear and disappear one by one on my screen. Even when my mother or father is not in them, I think, *She was alive then*, or *He was alive then*, or *They both were alive then*. I could still call them on the phone and talk to them, go down the hill from my house to theirs and see them, invite them to my house perched high on the hill for our weekly family dinners at the round table with the view my father loved and the light my mother loved, surrounded as it is by huge windows. The image of the glass dining room with my family in it now evokes a conservatory: a room that conserves the precious—our family as hothouse flowers. Or a sanctuary—a room that holds our family as it once was, loving and intact. Sometimes I think, as another photo appears, *That was only a month after my mother died*. Or, *That was two weeks before my father died*. It's like a test. The endless need to know, a toll, forever taxing. What was happening? Who was where?

"HE'S IN HEAVEN," I said.

We were talking about one of her older brothers, my first cousin. As we sat on the edge of the fountain in the front garden, the water caught the sunlight and tossed it back in sparkling diamonds that cascaded into the wide octagonal pool.

"¿Qué?" she asked, her smile turning quizzical.

I pointed to the sky, its usual summer blue. *"Está en el cielo."*

My little cousin laughed. *"¡Carlos!"* she called out. *"¡Dice que Eduardo está en el cielo! Eso no es verdad—¡está en Italia!"*

Another of her brothers, twelve, maybe thirteen years older than her, sat with our mothers closer to the house with its modern wall of windows and stucco frame. Hearing his little sister, he looked up, brow furrowed. Gazing across the lawn at us, his five-year-old sister and his ten-year-old cousin, he attempted a smile but said nothing.

No one had informed me that we were to hide the death of their brother from the younger children.

Several months earlier, my mother had held my hand, pulling me down the brick path from our house to the front gate, where the car waited. For some reason I have in my memory that I was wearing my white First Communion dress. It could be that my mother did put me in that dress for this particular occasion, because she was insisting I accompany her to the neighborhood church, where we would pray for the soul of her nephew, my cousin, dead at seventeen from a crash on the notoriously dangerous roads curving cliffside from the city of Lima to the suburban estates. Her sister's son had gone to heaven, she explained to me, her reluctant and complaining companion on this mournful outing. It was all very, very sad, and now we had to go and pray for God to welcome him and keep him safe for his mother.

I didn't really understand, and I don't remember what happened when we arrived at St. Anselm's, the small Catholic church on our street, where throughout my childhood my mother would sporadically take us to hear Mass from an old white priest. I just remember my mother's hand pulling mine, the white dress, the brick path.

ONCE MY GRANDMOTHER WAS visiting us in California from Peru, which she used to do every few years. We were taking a break from shopping at the local mall to sit in the courtyard at one of the small outdoor tables and eat something, probably pastries with coffee. Imagine an older lady, *una señora,* with her silver hair up in an elegant bun, wearing a long string of pearls around her neck and large pearl earrings, her fingers adorned with diamonds and her left wrist with gold bangles that, whenever she moves her hands, clink against an old watch she has worn for years—a watch that belonged to the grandson who died so long ago in that car crash in the far-flung suburbs of Lima.

As we sat drinking coffee and eating croissants, she said, "*Sabes,* if my siblings and my friends *están en el infierno,* if they are in hell right now, *no quiero ir al cielo*." She was thinking out loud about her love for her friends and her family. Heaven wouldn't be heaven for her if they weren't there. She preferred hell with her loved ones to heaven without them.

These were also the years when she would announce—often after talking about the sisters (she had seven) or friends (she had many) who had died before her at seventy-five, or eighty, or eighty-five—that very soon she too would be "*con los angeles*." Whenever she said this, about dying in the near future and going to be with the angels, she'd raise her hands and waggle her fingers toward the sky, all the while looking at me with a mischievous smile.

YEARS LATER, WHEN WE WERE visiting family in Lima, my mother and I sat in the back seat as my uncle drove us around so we could do our errands. My aunt sat in the front beside her husband, knitting. Suddenly, she wondered out loud if she had closed the window in the front room where my 103-year-old grandmother, an invalid for the last two years, lay back at home.

Imagine now an ancient woman. Her body has shrunk alarmingly. No longer does she smile or give anyone mischievous looks. She lies prone most of the day in the bed that the family moved to the living room so she would always be surrounded by life's daily commotion. Her hair, a dull gray, is gathered loosely in a clip rather than styled into a majestic, silvery bun. She sleeps most of the time and rarely speaks.

That day on our errands, my aunt worried about her catching a cold if a breeze came in through the open window in the living room. My mother answered by saying maybe it didn't matter so much if their mother caught a cold, since she was so old, and such an invalid. In fact, my grandmother had told her she badly wanted to die but couldn't—she was trapped *"en este cuerpo."*

I piped up from the back then, thinking it helpful to explain my mother's point of view in this particular case, as it was also mine. "You know, your cousin Jorge helped his mother when she wanted to die—because he's a geriatric doctor he could give her morphine for pain, and she just stopped eating one day."

My aunt digested this information, her knitting needles clicking furiously, as we stopped and started in the traffic of Lima's downtown. "Now I'm not going to be able to sleep all night thinking about how my cousin killed my aunt," she fretted. *"¡Carambas! Mi primo mató a mi tía."*

MY FATHER DIED LIKE MY great-aunt did, but with years more forethought and planning. And that was the way he wanted it. He was always a controlling person, rigid in his rules about a clean house: No shoes indoors, the dog must stay outside on the covered porch in its wooden house no matter the weather (rain, thunder, lightning), the household budget must be strictly maintained, with limited allowances for the entire family, including himself.

I was in my twenties and still living at home when I saw a book on the coffee table titled *Final Exit*. Intrigued but also apprehensive, I asked my father about it. He'd bought it, he told me, because it outlined effective ways to kill oneself. "What?" I asked. "Why?" He explained, for the first but not, as it turned out, the last time, that he would never accept living dependent on others, old and frail and helpless. His threshold for lack of independence was the inability to walk, to bathe and dress and feed himself. If the time came when that failure of self-sufficiency loomed near, he would commit suicide. By then his own father had fallen in the icy backyard at his house on the East Coast and been moved to a nursing home, where his mind declined rapidly for three years until he died, confused and alone.

At the time, still young, I questioned my father's confidence in his plans, despite the fact that, even then, a part of me agreed with his thinking.

Published in 1991, *Final Exit* is still in print, now in its third edition, and a *New York Times* bestseller.

MY FATHER AND I SIT TOGETHER IN the reverend's office, not in a church but in a hospital. I've driven him the fifteen minutes from his house to this hospital in Northern Marin, having agreed a few days prior to accompany him to this meeting. He had received earlier, in the mail, a hot pink sheet of paper to fill out. It's an "End-of-Life" or "Advanced Directive" document. There are many questions to answer: *Do you want to be resuscitated? Do you want artificial nutrition or hydration? Do you want comfort care or pain medication, even if it prolongs your life?* Etcetera, etcetera.

This meeting is instructive for me. I learn much about death and culture and belief systems. About inherent versus learned squeamishness and fear. It turns out that death tax looks different to different people from different cultures and religions and upbringings.

My father, I know, is excited to have been summoned to this meeting. To talk about his life and his death and how he wants to be treated in a medical emergency. He is also intrigued by the fact that this reverend who is talking to us from behind her desk in her hospital office is female. As a lifelong feminist and champion of girls and women always, I am gratified. As someone who grew up in a world where men and women stayed in their lanes, so to speak, with roles clearly defined by sex and gender, my father is fascinated.

He and I, both cerebral, both intellectual, ask many questions about the document itself as a cultural artifact as well as a series of practical questions that must be answered. The reverend tells us about the Wisconsin study where they piloted this exercise: the contemplating and answering of questions about end of life. We discuss the differences in culture, even within the United States, and she acknowledges that this initial study was very white, middle-class, and Midwestern.

At one point, the reverend asks about my mother. Why is she not here? She sees from the hospital records that my mother is also elderly and a member of this medical system.

My father and I both answer, knowing exactly why. My mother, Latina rather than Anglo, Catholic rather than Protestant, superstitious rather than atheist, cannot stand to think about death, to imagine the end of her life, to think about the particulars. She has only ever attended funerals reluctantly. She has never gone to her mother's grave to visit or to commune with the spirits or to meditate. She never took me to a single funeral when I was growing up. She wanted to protect her children from what she saw as depressing and morbid and possibly traumatizing. She was appalled when, at her uncle's open-casket funeral in Concord (to which she went very purposefully *without* her children), her aunt made each grandchild line up to kiss their grandfather's embalmed face. Meeting a reverend in a hospital to talk about the way she might want to die is not my mother's idea of a pleasant afternoon. I can see, however, that in many ways it is for my father, who believes that he can control his death if he tries hard enough, just as he made rigid routines of his daily life, sometimes at the expense of peace and calm at home with his wife and children.

This day with the reverend, we fill out the form with her. Sometimes I cut my father off and answer for him, knowing what he will say, what he wants for himself in the future if he is caught in a stroke or a heart attack. I want the same for myself. He only asks for clarification on one question—something about respiratory failure with pneumonia, and if the use of oxygen will save a life still worth living, will he want to receive this intervention?

It is the only box that she ticks off for him as "Yes."

A FEW HOURS BEFORE MY mother died, I sat by her hospital cot in my sister's house. I had pushed a chair as close as possible to her in order to more easily touch her, rub her fingers, smooth the skin on her arm, squeeze her hand. At one point my father sat beside me in stoic silence as I cried and touched my mother, who was silent in her dying, unable, by then, to open her eyes or communicate. Although I wasn't facing him and couldn't see him, I sensed my father's presence and knew he was sitting in the armchair next to me, his face pensive.

After a few minutes I felt something rest on my shoulder: his hand, the one with mangled and missing fingers from a long-ago mountain climbing accident. With my free hand I covered his damaged one, taking the unexpected comfort it offered. For the last time in this life, I held both my parents in the same moment.

THE SUMMER BEFORE MY MOTHER died, I drove with her and my younger son to my sister's house in Sacramento. We listened to a variety of music from my own collection—reggaeton, ABBA, classical—as we passed marshlands with egrets in the water and hawks in the sky, farms with cows grazing in the hot sun as it beat down on the rolling hills, then housing developments, malls, and dusty acreage with "For Sale" signs.

"Hay una canción bien linda que se llama 'Quiero Vivir'—¿crees que puedes buscarla ahorita para tocarla?"

My mother's request, to find a new song she'd recently discovered and play it in the car, was directed at her technologically savvy grandson in the back seat. He immediately took out his phone and started searching. He found a song with the same title and played the beginning for my mother—but no, it was a different version with a male singer and hers definitely had a woman singing, not a man.

In total, my son found three different versions before he landed on the one my mother had heard and fallen in love with, a lighter version, and sung by a woman's sweeter voice. In the end, my son put all four versions on my phone, where they remain.

THE FOLLOWING SUMMER, I DRIVE again with my mother to my sister's house in Sacramento. I look over at her as I steer the car on the long highway northeast toward the state capital. She looks happy. She's smiling and tapping her hand on her thigh to the beat of the music I've put on for her, knowing what she likes. We listen again and again to "Quiero Vivir"—the lighter version with the woman singing, the one she prefers. I believe she is happy to be in the car with me; to be going to her other daughter's house, where she might get better; to be having what she hopes may be a second chance at life. I know it from her smile and her conversation and the bright way, like a content and curious bird, that she looks around, out the window at the barns and silos, the clumps of cows under tight cliques of shady oaks, the marshes reflecting the blue of the sky dotted here and there with white clouds.

I don't know that this will be my last car ride with her.

Quiero vivir means *I want to live*.

About ten days after our car ride together, three days before her death, my mother and I find ourselves alone in my sister's house. My niece and nephew are at camp or dance class; my sister is perhaps running errands or at a work meeting. My own sons are at summer jobs an hour and a half away in our own county, located southwest of Sacramento. Even the dog is outside in the yard.

My bathrobed mother sits in her wheelchair. She is thin, so thin. For the last two months she has been slowly starving, the pounds finally (ironically!) melting away after almost an entire lifetime of yo-yo diets.

In the unusual quiet of the house, my mother turns to me. "*No quiero morir*," she says. "*Quiero vivir*."

MY MOTHER HAD BEEN GONE a month. The tax I'd paid since then was heavy. Sometimes I could barely stand under its weight.

My father chose this time to start giving me various articles from the house. "Make sure to take Grandma's plates the next time you're here," he said once. Another time, my brother entered my house ahead of our father one evening for our weekly family dinner carrying the heavy box of antique silverware my mother had always protected fiercely, counting the spoons after every dinner party.

"Why do you have that?"

"Dad made me bring it for you to keep."

After my father negotiated the transfer of three or four of this type of household article, I said to him, "Dad! Just because Mom's gone doesn't mean you have to empty the house. You're still living there!"

A thought entered my head.

"Wait—are you thinking of doing your final exit plan? I thought you were going to warn us before."

"Consider yourself warned."

RECENTLY, IN MADRID'S MUSEO Nacional del Prado, I saw my father. I saw him in a portrait by the Spanish Baroque painter Jusepe de Ribera.

It wasn't really my father, of course, who has been dead over a year, but the painted visage is so similar to his it's as if Ribera used his aged face as a model for this portrait of a saint. The room was hung all around with paintings by Ribera, Goya, and El Greco. Ribera, as I commented to the friend walking around the museum with me, surely did love his saints. There were so many old saints, all men, depicted as reflecting into the middle distance, receiving a vision from above, or dying. The one who had my father's ninety-three-year-old face was Jerome, wearing a single, toga-like garment draped across his skinny shoulder. A skull sat by him, representing, as the plaque next to the ornate frame claimed in Spanish and then English, his ascetic two years in the desert searching for peace.

My atheist father was definitely not a saint, but he *was* measured in all things, including food and drink. He took walks and worked in his garden until a week before his death. He was an intellectual, with texts including Japanese history, Western philosophy, and the great works of English and American literature sitting on the living room bookshelf that spanned an entire wall. Jerome, considered the most learned of the saints, spent his life reading, translating, and weighing in on moral debates.

My father appeared to be there, in front of me, mere feet away from me. His close-cropped hair, only ever washed with bar soap and brushed forward; his broad forehead, his bushy eyebrows, his long, thin nose, his white beard. Yet he was not there; he was gone, unreachable, untouchable.

I felt the tax of finality press on my shoulders, the back of my neck. I could not talk to him and know he'd hear me; I could not touch him and know he'd feel me; I could not explain to him and know he'd understand.

At one point I stepped closer to Ribera's painting, closer to my father's face, extending a finger toward the canvas, eager to show my friend a trick of brushstroke or an inspired use of color. In my peripheral vision, I saw a black-uniformed docent, official ID lanyarded around her neck, leap from her chair.

"¡No tocar!"

I SIT ON A BENCH WITH A visiting friend and my heart hurts. It's that familiar pain, a little dulled a year after my mother's death but still weighing on me, unrelenting. It's a bright, sunny day with just a bit of breeze—a fresh breeze tinged with salt from the ocean in front of us. My friend and I have come especially to this seaside town in my county, a fifteen-minute drive from my house. We've been close for decades, since freshman year at our all-girls Catholic high school.

We sit companionably, side by side, gazing at the blue-green ocean and the silvery white city and the rusty red bridge. Ferries come and go, pelicans and seagulls fly about, and visitors stroll with their tiny fluffy dogs up and down the path that closely borders the coastline. Our conversation drifts like chaff or straw on the surface of the water, this way and that, from past to present to future and back again.

I've chosen this location for our afternoon outing not only because it's beautiful, with San Francisco framed by Angel Island, Belvedere, and the Golden Gate, but also because by sitting in this precise location—on a bench, beside the curving path that meanders gently along the edge of the bay—I can pay homage to my mother. She loved this town, this view, this path, the sky and the sun and the sea. I sat with her many times on one of these benches, looking at the waves and the birds and the boats, at the city across the bay silver and white against the sky.

I tell my friend about my thoughts. How I know my mother would have loved to be with us right now, on this bench, observing the locals as well as the visitors and tourists as they pass by, a moving panorama. "I feel so sad," I say, "because a few times in the last couple of years she called and asked me if I wanted to come here with her, and I usually said no, because I thought I was too busy."

My friend turns her head toward me as she contemplates what I've said. She tells me it's normal to have these feelings of sadness laced with guilt, or with frustration for not doing things differently, before it's too late. Her father died five years ago—a man so kind, so refined, a soft-spoken man, a gentle man. In his last months, his deteriorating mind prompted him to ask his daughter if she would sleep in his room. "Will you stay with me tonight?" he'd ask, afraid of the darkness, of the emptiness that had morphed for him into a threatening solitude.

But no, she rarely had the patience to keep him company through the long, quiet hours of what had become for him the lonely night. She tells me that instead she'd go off, impatient, wanting a break, wanting time with her husband or on her own, to rest, to watch television, to sleep, to unwind. Not wanting to answer the constant questions or block the inappropriate demands of a sometimes querulous, always needy father. And she feels regret, still, after five years. "Now I want so badly to go back in time and stay with him. But I can't."

I tell her how I thought, I *believed*, I had at least ten good years left with my mother. Years that I planned to fill with drives and bench sitting, with view gazing and clothes shopping, with tea drinking and trips to Lima to visit my aunt, her beloved sister. "In my mind I was so sure that I would be able to catch up and be with her more. Because I knew my children would both be in college, and I would finally have time to spend with her."

But fate cheated me. Life asked of me a sacrifice that I didn't want to give. Death demanded of me a tax I did not want to pay. I was forced to give up a future with my mother. And she will never come back. She was not spared at the last minute, as was Isaac, nor will she resurrect, as did Lazarus, or Jesus himself.

"At least," I add, trying to be cheerful, trying to be positive like my mother always was, "she would be so happy to know that we're here together."

I'M STILL IN MADRID WITH my friend, visiting my son during his semester abroad. This afternoon he's at the Universidad Carlos III de Madrid, and will meet us later in the evening, after his classes are over and he can take the bus to have dinner with us at a restaurant in one of the city's many plazas. My friend and I wander about, strolling from museum to café to the steps that lead up to a grand, empty conservatory from the fin de siècle era in the Parque de Madrid. The day is warm and humid, and tourists like us are everywhere, eager to take in as much Spanish culture as possible. In front of the glass conservatory is a trio of musicians, young people, two of them playing violins and one a cello. They play a favorite of mine, Pachelbel's Canon in D. My friend knows I love this piece, and she suggests we sit on the steps with the other park visitors to listen to the music among the trees.

As we settle down, arranging beside us our bags full of booty from the museum gift shop, a couple from the audience steps out in front of the musicians to dance an impromptu dance, a beautiful, lyrical, graceful dance, the man twirling and holding and following his partner as she sways and dips and turns.

I know immediately that my mother would adore this moment: the city, the park, the trees, and the grand old conservatory, the audience spontaneously gathered on the stone steps, the music and the dancers. After she went to Greece with a group of adventurers, on her own and in her eighties, she showed me a video she'd taken of two of her fellow travelers, one of them a pretty young woman, who spontaneously stood up to dance salsa in harmonious tandem at a restaurant where they were all eating dinner. My mother was so pleased with this video, with the spontaneity and the guitar and the clapping, that she wanted me to see it often, to have me take the same pleasure in watching it as she did.

My friend films the man and the woman dancing in the middle of the park in Madrid, obviously expert dancers, moving so gracefully to music my mother loved as much as I did. She sends the video to me so that I have it on my own phone. Every time I play even a few seconds of it in the weeks and months to come, I will have this urge to send it to my mother so that she too can partake in the pleasure of the music and the movement. But of course I cannot. The time for seeing through my mother's eyes, for judging events by her standards, the time for sharing moments and sights I know she would enjoy, is over.

My soul protests this tax as excessive, the toll as too heavy. I no longer have her as a sturdy backdrop to my own experiences and reactions; she is no longer there as standard bearer, as prism of reality, as sharer of beautiful spontaneous dancing in Spanish parks or Greek restaurants.

My FATHER DIES THREE MONTHS after my mother. Many of my friends immediately assume it's because he was heartbroken after his wife's passing, desolate and adrift without her. They want it to be one of those poignant, tender stories where a couple, married over fifty years, cannot live without the other.

"No," I correct each of them. "That was definitely not the case!"

My father dies because his strength has begun to ebb dramatically. He knows he will soon be too weak to do his morning calisthenics, drag the two garbage bins down the long driveway once a week, clean the kitchen floor with the wet rag he's proudly repurposed from a worn-out bath towel, pick himself up after one of his middle-of-the-night falls in the bathroom, cook for himself, dress himself, walk.

My father dies the way he promised. Several times in the past decade he told me, "I'm not leaving this house except in a pine box." He delivered on this promise, except that he left in a plastic body bag instead of a wooden coffin.

My father dies because he wants to. He was finding it harder and harder to walk, mobility his personal test for life being worthwhile. When our dog was run over by a car and the vet informed us that the expensive operation he needed to save his life would not guarantee him the ability to walk or run, my father chose to have him put down. When we didn't yet know that my mother was already dying, my father told me she shouldn't live if she would never walk again.

My father dies by choice. He dies on the day and at the time he chooses. He dies from the poison the hospital sent to his house by courier.

My father dies after I play "Für Elise" for him over and over on the downstairs piano, knowing it is his favorite piece. He dies after his children gather around him as he lies on his bed wearing, incongruously, a bright blue hoodie. He dies after he takes the two antiemetics a half hour before the potion. He dies after I tell him about the legacy I've inherited from him—a love of walks. He dies after taking the poison, holding the coffee mug with both hands and complaining briefly of its bitter taste. He dies after I stand from the chair I've been sitting on at the foot of his bed and hug him, telling him how much we love him. He dies after I arrange his pillows more comfortably under his head, adjusting the hood of his blue sweatshirt. He dies after I lie beside him on the edge of the bed, my hand upon his. He dies after his heart slows, then speeds up, then slows again. He dies after I rub his hand, press gently on his chest to feel his heartbeat, smooth his forehead. He dies after I cry silently next to him. He dies when his heart finally stops.

I'M BY MYSELF. DRIVING SOUTH TO Los Angeles. Listening to my music. "Quiero Vivir," my mother's song, comes on, picked at random from the shuffled playlist. What to do? I want to fast-forward to another song, one not fraught with tax and grief, one that won't send me back to the stabbing anguish of her death—*What's happening? Where am I? Where are you?*

But this time I don't. I decide to lean into the pain, even though it feels like I'm cracking my ribs open for it. I give in to the memories, and find my mother once again as the woman with the sweet voice she loved sings, over and over, *Quiero vivir*.

The Window

I HALF SAT, HALF LAY ON the modern and capacious sectional. Although impressive in size, this sofa was plain—no tufts, no brass tacks, no curves or wooden accents. Instead it was a cool gray, without pattern, in a simple geometrical shape. While my legs stretched out before me on the sectional, one hand rested protectively on my still-tender stomach.

Forty-five minutes earlier, I had gathered with my husband, his mother, and our younger son in the kitchen of my brother-in-law's house in San Francisco, the city across the Golden Gate from our own home in Marin County. The kitchen is a narrow galley at the back, typical of Victorian-era houses. We'd finished the Indian takeaway that my sister-in-law, previous to our arrival, had graciously picked up and carefully set out on the counter as a kind of impromptu buffet from which to serve ourselves before sitting at the table in the corner. The eldest of my in-laws' two daughters opened a couple of packages of Petit Écolier cookies and I, happy to be included in this warm family get-together, helped place them on a large plate in the middle of the table to share for dessert. As the conversation continued around me, I nibbled the edges of a dark chocolate–covered biscuit.

At one point, soon after the nibbling began, I felt a familiar discomfort in my belly. I knew from experience that it signaled stomach upset. I waited a few more moments, nibbling on a second cookie, hoping the flash of discomfort would go away, having been but a false alarm. I didn't want to be forced to leave the table, to leave the conversation and the laughter and the sharing of food, even though my Syrian mother-in-law seemed to be in one of her quiet and distant moods, at least toward me. Time proved differently, however, and I announced my need to use the restroom, sliding off the bench seat after my husband obligingly stood up to let me get by.

Five, ten, then twenty minutes later found me still in the guest bathroom. I had no phone with me because I'd left it at home, and I hadn't thought to grab my reading glasses and a magazine before bolting the brass lock to barricade myself behind the bathroom door. My mood vacillated between boredom and worry that my in-laws might think it was their food that had caused my stomach distress.

As I waited, I looked around me. I noted the trendiness of the powder room's wallpaper, a trendiness matching the deep blue varnish of the door. This wallpaper had a vibrant color palette, vivid greens and oranges and reds, in a mysterious tropical flower pattern. A William Morris run amok? The toilet roll holder, the faucet and handles, the sconces, even the light switch were, like the aforementioned bolt lock, a heavy, rich brass. Conversely, the sink was a hard block of white marble with gray veins, its cold color and slick texture incongruous, to me, among all the lavish warmth of the door and the brass and the wallpaper. If this was a picture in a magazine with the caption, "What doesn't belong here?" I would point directly to the sink. On the right side of this sink, my sister-in-law or her decorator had placed a variety of luxury soaps and perfumes—rich, expensive, European. On the left was an orange leather napkin holder, offering thick matching orange napkins. That night with stomach issues, my attention stayed with this napkin holder for a while.

The high quality of the leather and the deep shade of the orange, more elegant than garish, told me it was Hermès—that old French company that started with leather equestrian goods, saddles and saddlebags and boots, and now makes scarves and Birkins and cuffs that are coveted around the world for their quality and status. I wondered about the napkins. Could they too be Hermès? They were the same deep orange, thick and luxurious to the touch.

Contemplating this, I was reminded that those napkins were appropriate only for the drying of newly washed and perfumed hands, and glanced at the toilet roll holder. Oh no—the roll had thinned dangerously.

The modern block of marble that was the sink disallowed any functional cupboard or drawer for the keeping of bathroom essentials. Peering underneath anyway, hoping against hope, I saw only a single drainpipe, which was, no surprise here, made of a heavy brass.

Fortunately for me, my husband knocked at the door around the same time I realized I was running out of toilet paper and would be left with the inappropriately thick and expensive Hermès-orange paper napkins.

"Are you okay?" he called from outside.

"Yeah, I just have a stomachache."

"That's too bad . . . Can I get you anything?"

"Actually—I need some more toilet paper!"

I could hear my husband as he headed back toward the kitchen, the sound of his footsteps receding as he crossed the massive foyer off of which, under a low-ceilinged nook, was ensconced the little powder room where I continued to wait, now for the replenishment of much-needed supplies as well as final resolution to my stomach situation.

After a bit I heard above me, on the second floor of this tall four-story house, much stomping of feet and running about from hall to room to hall. I wondered who it was, as I doubted very much that this could be my husband hurrying so noisily to do my bidding.

About a minute afterward, there was a knock, and my sixteen-year-old niece announced her presence. I clutched my pashmina to my chest so that it covered the tops of my thighs as I reached forward from my seat and slid open the bolt, but, as it turns out, I did so unnecessarily. My niece made sure to turn her head as she handed me a fresh roll of toilet paper. "Here you go, Auntie."

My very being flooded with warmth and tender affection. All because of the "Auntie," all because of the considerate turning of the head, all because of this errand on my behalf, this favor to me. My niece had been sent to get more toilet paper, and she had hurried to do it, and she had considered my privacy as I sat exposed with nowhere to hide, and she had called me "Auntie."

Some context for the flush of gratitude that attended my niece's handing over of a roll of toilet paper through a partially opened door with a gaze carefully averted: "Auntie" is a common moniker for actual aunts as well as older women within the family or even within the larger community in certain cultures, including Syria's. It's a soft title, almost an endearment, at least in my understanding. It signifies a sense of belonging to a family, a community, a culture. And although I am not Syrian or Arab or Middle Eastern, I love much of the culture I married into and that marks, in part, the identity of my sons.

This niece who had just run upstairs and galloped around to find and fetch toilet paper for me, who had politely looked away from my helpless body vulnerable on the toilet seat, and who had called me "Auntie," was the same niece who had, when a year ago I tried to put my arm around her, flinched. All these months later, I recalled the moment vividly, bright like a flash suffused with disappointment and alienation. I react badly to flinches, being hyperaware of them, trying to understand them with analysis and dissection and endless rememberings of the flinch itself. Its trigger—what about me was distasteful? Its nature—length, overtness, deliberateness. Its context—place and date and time. Rumination and remembering. Again and again.

That previous year, when my niece flinched away from my touch, I'd felt she was rejecting me. Rejection, after all, is part of any flinch. A flinch can signify a moment of revulsion or a lifetime of hatred. In this case, I imagined she found my age, or my generation, or my status as an in-law somehow distasteful. It was automatic, and may have been the reaction of a teenager to being touched by an adult. But I feared the distaste of the young for the old, of the current for the outdated, of the growing, nubile body for the flesh that has started to deteriorate. I feared that the distaste was a rejection of the body and therefore, on some primal level, the self.

I've read that the peak of a person's physicality is at sixteen, after which the body begins its inevitable descent into decay. My niece was fifteen the year of her flinch, and sixteen the year of her anti-flinch. I'm sure the memory of the flinch and the many unpackings and deconstructions of it that followed took a part in the flush of well-being, of happy gratitude, I felt at her anti-flinch—her favor to me, her consideration, her use of the name "Auntie."

When I felt it safe to leave my prison, my cocoon, I washed my hands with the expensive and perfumed soap, drying them with an orange napkin. But I only made it across the foyer on my way to the kitchen before I decided it would be a good idea to lie down on the couch, that modern sofa in cool gray, in preparation for rejoining the party still chatting at the table. At this point, even though I imagined my brother-in-law had served his usual Arab-style mint tea, which I love, to sip from delicate glass cups imported from the Middle East, I wasn't ready to partake in this after-dinner ritual.

There I half lay, half sat on the sectional in a room by myself, my legs stretched out before me and one hand resting protectively on a stomach that, for the last forty-five minutes or so, had been struggling to recalibrate.

As I reclined on the sofa, tired out and resting, I observed my surroundings just as I had earlier observed the inside of the powder room. This space was situated to the right of the huge foyer, and had been remodeled as a kind of transitional room. Many people would consider this space a family room, yet with one side completely open to the foyer and the front door, it felt too transitional, too in-between and limbo-like to merit such a warm and cozy name. It seemed an appropriate place for me to rest, though, after the private, isolated bathroom and before the social brightness of the kitchen. Someone, the designer or my sister-in-law, had decided to decorate this particular space in cool blues, grays, and whites. There was the gray sofa, the white throw pillows that matched the soft white area rug, the framed black-and-white portraits of my brother-in-law's family, complete with fluffy white lapdog. To my left was the missing wall, the cavernous foyer, the large formal salon.

My gaze wandered idly around the room, and I noticed for the first time a small square window situated in a corner beside the large television with its glowing screen saver of a blue, gray, and white impressionist painting. This window is a real window, clear-paned, and through it I could see into the larger window of the kitchen. My view from the couch was direct and unimpeded—no trick of light and shadow or of deliberately angled mirrors. I listened as I looked, for I found I could hear the conversation, almost intact, which emanated from the group in the kitchen. As I heard the sounds of my husband's hearty laughter and my sister-in-law's commentary and my niece's joke-telling, I could see through the small square window the back of my husband's head (big, shiny, bald) and his mother's—small, held rigidly erect, with snow-white hair pinned up.

"I do not like Marin," I suddenly heard uttered in my mother-in-law's heavy and formal accent. "If it was not for my son, I would never accept living there. It is so small, and—excuse me—the people are not sophisticated." After she had been widowed some years earlier, her two children, my husband and his brother, had convinced her to downsize from her mansion in Atherton to a smaller house a mere two minutes from our home in Marin County.

I felt the familiar pang of rejection. Such contempt in so few words. I couldn't help but take it personally, even after all these years, because I considered Marin and our small town at its heart to have been my true home for most of my life. I loved it passionately and unreservedly. The redwoods and the oaks, the mountain, the bay, the creeks, the trails, both Stanford and Berkeley within an hour's drive, Napa's and Sonoma's vineyards nearby, the beauty of San Francisco in view across the iconic bridge . . . Yet my mother-in-law dismissed it all, quickly and with disdain.

I heard my younger son try to defend Marin, the only home he can remember. "But it's so pretty there." He is a favorite of his *teta,* and knows how to approach the dragon carefully—how to engage without conflict, how to poke back without wounding. I don't know if I would have had the energy to mount a defense, however brief, after so many years of hearing my hometown abused in my mother-in-law's superior tones. Although I couldn't see her face and didn't hear her reply to her grandson, I can imagine the dismissive upward nod of head with which she responded to him. I've seen it enough times myself.

A few more minutes passed, and I remained on the couch in a kind of meditative state, as if I were floating in a cool blue pool. I'd dimmed the lights before lying down so that the room resembled an underwater aquarium. Now I rested, a passive listener, no conversational effort required of me, no acceptable expression to arrange on my face in reaction to whatever was said at the table.

Then I heard my mother-in-law again—this time she was directing her speech at my husband. They must have been talking around the kitchen table about the differences between my husband and his brother, who was his father's golden boy until the father died. It seems like my mother-in-law has taken up the torch these days, because she makes sure to shed its light onto her younger son at every opportunity.

According to my mother-in-law, this son speaks Arabic better (indeed, he has a golden tongue in several languages), and is more agreeable, more charming, more sophisticated in general. I've seen her face light up when he phones her, and whenever he enters a room her attention becomes more focused and her demeanor more relaxed. She argues with her older son, my husband, when he wants something different from his younger brother for the table at a restaurant. She insists that whatever the younger brother wants, he should get. His desires are always and already good and right and perfect. My husband is second best, the taken-for-granted, always-there son, the cloudy day to his brother's brilliant sky, the tarnished silver to his brother's gleaming platinum.

"And you did not even marry an Arab."

Whoa. I sat up from my relaxed position in the cool blue room with its soft shadows. After knowing me for thirty-four years, after being related to me as my mother-in-law for thirty years, after receiving from me her first grandchildren, after watching me prove my love for her son and my loyalty to their family over and over, I was suddenly—*again*—the outsider, the imposter and the interloper, unappreciated and unwanted?

WHEN HE WAS MY BOYFRIEND, my husband didn't introduce me to his parents for the first four years of our relationship, fearing their active and vocal disapproval. Once during this time, we were in the city together and he had to leave me to meet his parents. Because he didn't want a forced introduction, he dropped me off to wait for my mother to come by and pick me up.

When she arrived a few minutes later, my mother saw what I didn't: her daughter abandoned on a street corner, standing awkwardly alone, in public, waiting. She chastised me for allowing such treatment from a man. I resisted with denial and defensiveness. But now that I am much older, a mother myself and an aunt and mentor to younger women, I see what she saw.

A few months after we did finally meet, I remember waiting by my boyfriend's parents' parked car in the city, saying good night after dinner at a restaurant, watching as they prepared to get in and drive away. His father stood by the door, keys in hand, wearing his usual three-piece suit, which included jacket, vest, and tie. We must have been talking, arguing—at least on his side—about religion, their family's being Islam, mine a loose South American Catholicism. *You should convert and become a Muslim if you are going to be with a Syrian boy!* was his parting shot before he climbed into the Range Rover and slammed the door.

On a road trip to Seattle to look into his residency program, my boyfriend and his parents argued all the way up Highway 5. He had just informed them that he wanted to get married to me—the Catholic, Peruvian and American, English- and Spanish-speaking girlfriend. In other words, the non-Muslim, non-Syrian, non-Arabic-speaking girlfriend. The wrong girlfriend, and the unhoped-for, unplanned-for, undreamed-of fiancée. There was shouting in the car, according to my boyfriend, and also throwing of telephones in the hotel room. His father and mother definitely did not want me to marry their son; they did not want me in their family; they did not want me as their daughter-in-law.

There was once an ideal daughter-in-law for my husband's parents, if not the ideal wife for my husband. She existed in the flesh before my husband and I were first introduced at a nightclub in San Francisco. Her name was Yasmine, and he met her within the Arab Muslim community. She was Syrian, spoke Arabic fluently, and practiced, as had her family for centuries and generations, Islam. She was also rich: For the year they were engaged, after she moved up to Palo Alto to be near her fiancé and attend the local community college, she routinely flew back down to Los Angeles with two empty suitcases in order to fill them with purchases made on Rodeo Drive. She also didn't wash her own hair; instead, she had weekly appointments at the beauty salon.

Eventually, a couple of months before he and I met, my husband broke off his engagement because of this materialism. When I was temporarily living with my in-laws in their house in Atherton, I came across a set of old photo albums in a drawer of the office we used as a playroom for our two sons. This album was dedicated to photos of the former fiancée, pretty, brown-haired, and checking all the right boxes: Syrian—check, Muslim—check, fluent in Arabic—check, from a wealthy family—check. Why did they keep this album, most definitely outdated, obsolete now within their family history, as a kind of hidden shrine to a wifely persona they idealized for their eldest son? Why did they fail, at the very least, to remove it from a room I was to inhabit for a full three years as their actual, living and breathing daughter-in-law?

There's also a smaller moment, yet one I remember still. A year after my introduction to his parents, my boyfriend called me early one morning to invite me to a restaurant in Palo Alto, near their home. They would be meeting his uncle for brunch. I'd never met this uncle before. Although the reservation was in just an hour, I thought I could make it if I hurried. I quickly dressed, got in our family car, drove down 101, across the bridge, through the city, and down 280, until finally I reached the exit for University Avenue. After circling the block several times to find parking, locking the car, and rushing into the restaurant, I found them finishing their meal. They hadn't waited for me to arrive. Only the uncle made an attempt to apologize in the midst of this, our first introduction.

"*La primera vez que conocí a tus abuelos*, your grandma put a photograph of your father's former wife, *la ex-esposa*, in the middle of the coffee table. Right in front of me. *A propósito*." It seems I was fated, in my own way, to live what my mother lived. Growing up, I heard her stories, time and again, of being told, not always in words, that she was an outsider, an interloper. As a Peruvian woman whose first language was Spanish, who spoke English with an accent, who didn't go to college, who was more dark than fair, she was the unwanted, the unhoped-for, the disdained second daughter-in-law to my father's parents.

Twelve years and two children after my marriage to their son, when I lived with my small family in my in-laws' Atherton home for three years, trying to save money to buy our own house in the ultra-expensive Bay Area, one of their two maids, a woman originally from Guatemala, advised my own mother in the Spanish they spoke to each other, "You need to get your daughter away from here. *La tratan muy mal.*"

EVENTUALLY I DID LEAVE MY shadowy blue grotto to go back into the kitchen, the space bright with food and talk I'd been looking at through the small window I'd never noticed before, connected randomly by sight and sound yet alone in my own darkened limbo. My mood had shifted again; I went back feeling different thrice over than when I left. First the stomach pain and the immediate need for privacy; then the rush of gratitude and the sense of belonging that accompanied my niece and the toilet roll handover; then, finally, another reminder that my husband's mother and father, my children's grandparents, had never fully accepted me.

A question that remains: Will my widowed mother-in-law—eighty-six years old now, thin and fragile and white-haired, living down the street from us but solitary nonetheless, still praying five times a day, still fasting during Ramadan, still eschewing bacon and wine—ever fully accept me?

Sadly, I know the answer. Stepping back and looking at the larger picture, my mother-in-law missed an opportunity to bond with her daughter-in-law over their shared experiences as two outsiders in various, sometimes conflicting, cultures—American, Syrian, Peruvian, Spanish, Arabic, Catholic, and Muslim, national and linguistic and religious. To bond over our shared feminism, our intellectual strengths, and our fierce motherhood. I no longer have the luxury of an expansive future, of years and decades to come during which I might hope for a better relationship with her. My thirty-first wedding anniversary is next month; she is eighty-six, and I am fifty-six; her first grandchildren, my sons, are both fully grown now. The truth—that my mother-in-law will never change—is the unhappily-ever-after ending I have to accept.

White Bitch

THIS STORY CONTAINS SQUABS and slogans and even a gun, but unlike Chekhov's, it appears when it appears, only once and with no foreshadowing. Where to start? I think with the squabs. They, after all, were there from the beginning.

THE RESTAURANT GLEAMED WITH wealth and privilege. Or so it seemed to me, a woman in my early twenties, only a year out of a large public university where, in contrast to a sophisticated foodie, I'd looked forward with inordinate enthusiasm to the cafeteria burgers and bulk-mix chocolate cake. At this fancy restaurant, in polar opposition to my dorm's dining hall, the tablecloths were white and heavy, the brass accents burnished and shining, the velvet-backed chairs a plush moss green.

I leaned over my menu toward my companion, a young man my age, not a boyfriend but a companion nonetheless in seeking adventures in San Francisco, the city we both loved. "What should I get?"

I'm known for my food envy—if someone at my table ordered steak and I chose chicken (this was years before I saw the wisdom of vegetarianism), I invariably coveted the juicy meat while disdaining my ordinary fowl.

"I don't know," he said, "what looks good?"

We discussed the menu back and forth until we decided we'd both get the squab.

As we waited for our meal, I took in the atmosphere—gleaming, polished, luxe in that eighties way that still lingered into the beginning of the nineties, and the clientele—older, certainly than us, and also presupposing in gold jewelry and coiffured hair and proper dinner jackets. There's an old image on the internet of the owner-chef, Jeremiah Tower, talking to a table of luncheoning ladies who are, every single one, blonde and sleekly styled, wearing shades of white and cream and beige. The lighting that evening in 1992 was warm and subtle, the silverware solid and heavy, the fine wine glasses large and delicate. I'm sure my companion and I were conversing easily, as we always did, gossiping and commenting in general, as well as analyzing our surroundings. He wore the required jacket, a dark blue in his case, and I wore my favorite "posh" outfit: high heels, silk skirt, fitted Italian blazer bought heavily discounted from the famed Back Room of Loehmann's (my mother's and my favorite store).

Sometime later—a good twenty minutes, I'd say—we began to wonder when our dinner was coming. I was looking forward to my squab, not realizing it would be a finicky meal, with small bones to wrestle only for the meager harvest of a few mouthfuls of tender flesh. We'd long finished our salads and were growing impatient for our entrées to complement well-mannered sips of wine when the *clang! clang! clang!* of ladle on pot forced our attention to a corner of the room near the kitchen, where stood the chef in a stained apron and floppy toque.

As he began to speak, two waiters appeared at our table, each carrying a serving of squab, and deftly placed them in front of us. Momentarily distracted, I glanced down at my plate, noting its wide, shiny-clean rim and, in the middle, the little browned squab glistening on its pile of exotic vegetables.

"I have an announcement!" Jeremiah Tower called out. "I've just been notified that there's a group of protesters coming up Van Ness from Market. We don't know how it's going to turn out, but in light of the riots in LA yesterday, I want to give you the chance to leave the restaurant now. No need to settle your bill." Then, after a short pause, "You can also stay if you choose."

My companion and I looked at each other. This was unexpected.

"What do you want to do?" he asked me.

We had both seen the video of the policemen beating a prone Rodney King; we had both watched the riots erupt in LA following the verdict exonerating those same policemen. We had felt outrage at the beating, and recognized the video as proof of police brutality against Black Americans. We looked down at our matching squabs, each untouched and looking succulent. I wanted to go. There was no way of telling if the still-small group coming together in anger at flagrant injustice would morph into a full-blown chaos of looting and burning. I had also seen the beating by rioters in LA of the hapless white truck driver, caught in the wrong place at the wrong time.

We stood—abandoning our entrées, pushing our chairs away from the table, dropping napkins by dinner plates—and joined the other nervous customers exiting the double glass doors.

Because we were parked off of Van Ness Avenue, we had to walk a couple of blocks to our car. My companion grabbed my hand as we hurried along one side of the street, as far away as possible from the protesters who increased in number the farther away we walked from the restaurant. More and more people, mostly young men, crowded the street as we neared our parking place. We continued to hurry, almost running, as we approached the car.

Finally, out of breath, we jumped in and locked ourselves inside.

As we drove between the parking lot's gates, my companion reached under his seat and drew out a gun. "Here, take this."

I'd never held a gun before, and I noticed, despite the anxiety and the stress and the fear, that it was heavy for such a small thing. Compact and black, it weighed in my palm, and I was aware of the effort it took to hold it steady above my lap. "What do you want me to do? I don't know anything about guns!"

Turning onto the street, he said, "Wave it around in front of the window if anyone comes up to us."

Okay . . . I thought to myself. *I guess I could do that.* But I fervently hoped that no one would approach us, that I wouldn't have to pretend I was ready to use such a weapon.

Could I, though? I mean, should I? I looked again at the gun in my hand—black, blunt, solid, and dense. *Yes*, I thought, *I could*. I could wave it around in front of the closed car window, exploiting it for its reputation and thus avoiding the possibility of anyone, including my companion, using it. I thought about the explosive violence in LA, Rodney King's broken face, the shattered glass of immigrant storefronts, the fires everywhere. I thought about the people we'd passed on the way to the car, walking, not really marching, definitely not running or charging—at least not yet—up Van Ness Avenue. I thought about the man across the street traveling in the opposite direction from us as we left the restaurant. I thought about how he'd spotted me, hurrying past in heels and silk, and how, despite my black hair curling down my back, my olive skin, my red lipstick and hoop earrings, he'd looked directly at me and yelled—*White bitch!*

Hair

ALL AROUND ME ALL I SEE is brown hair, black hair, curly hair. I'm surrounded by it. Some of the hair I see is long, spiraling down backs; some of it is short, twisting up from foreheads, crimping close to necks; some is layered, with waves filling out bobs or ringlets shaping shoulder-length styles. My own reflection in the mirror facing me shows similar hair—deep black and curly all over, in some places ringleted and in others irritatingly frizzy.

The inside of this salon is decorated eclectically, with seemingly no theme except perhaps for a general non-Western ethnicness. There's a potted bamboo in one corner and a statue of the Buddha next to it. I contemplate, when I'm not observing the patrons and stylists and their hair, a column in the middle of the room adorned with a tiny Persian prayer rug and a small blue evil eye beneath it. Sandalwood incense burns quietly on the reception counter. Of course there's the usual salon paraphernalia—mirrors everywhere, shelves displaying products for sale (in this case moisturizing shampoo, curl-enhancing gel, and mousse to put shine on the most kinky of locks), glass containers full of blue water for the sanitation of combs and brushes and scissors, the black-and-chrome chairs, on one of which I sit.

What about the outside of this salon? Where is it located? How did I find it? I found out about it through the grapevine made up of curly-haired women. It is nondescript, so much so that I never noticed it before on a street I've been familiar with my whole adult life. On this street known for preppy clubs, expensive Italian, French, and American restaurants, designer boutiques and trendy gift shops, the salon is an oasis—small, almost hidden in a desert of mainstream white hegemony.

MY HAIR HISTORY: PAINFUL TUGGING, torturous detangling, quiet crying, toxic chemicals, rain-paranoia and moisture-phobia, oversized rollers, hours under a dryer, experiments with primitive hair irons, default use of scarves and kerchiefs, hatred of humidity, gratitude for the dryness of an airplane cabin, and, always, the naïve hope that I might achieve pretty hair.

MY AUNT HAD "GOOD" HAIR. Her sister, my mother, had "bad" hair. There were only the two of them, both girls, born close together in time and brought up almost as twins. Thus my mother grew up with this constant reminder of what her hair could have been like if it wasn't for a twist of DNA, a kink in her particular set of genes. Because I'm sure she did see it as a twist or a kink—a deviation on her side of the genetic pool, not her sister's. My aunt's hair was perfect, ideal. Thick and glossy and straight. She could run her fingers through it and it always fell back into perfect place. She would need only to brush it roughly in the morning and could either air- or blow-dry it after a shower; the processes of washing and drying and styling, so complicated and time-consuming for my mother and me, were for my aunt always simple and easy.

My mother loved the glossy black hair of Japanese women. The way it could hang like shining sheets on either side of their faces, down their backs. She often recalled, with a nostalgic fondness, the beauty of her best friend's hair during the years when they were young and lay on the beach or swam in the water every chance they got. The way Clotilde would emerge from the waves with her blonde hair, long and sleek, flowing from her head and over her shoulders and down her back. No bangs, no flip, no layers. One shining whole.

When I was older and would hear my mother recount her envy when watching Clotilde surf and sunbathe with her silky, effortlessly beautiful hair, I started to imagine a James Bond actress in a swimsuit—beautiful, sophisticated, and chic even in the ocean or on the beach, even with the compounded challenges to ideal hair of water, wind, and sand. My mother envied her friend's hair, her sister's hair. The *straightness*. The straightness that was the opposite of kinky, of bent, the opposite of deviant.

What about me? Reader, I swallowed the narrative whole. I internalized all of it. Lock, stock, and barrel, kit and caboodle. The envy of others' straight hair, the frustration with my own frizzy hair, the despair of ever being free from worry and vigilance (*constant vigilance!*) when it came to humidity, to drizzle, mist, or rain, to swimming anywhere, anytime.

ONCE, NOT TOO LONG AGO, after I'd turned fifty in fact, an acquaintance and I were talking about hair when she stopped me mid-complaint. "Why are you so obsessed with these minute details?" she asked me. She went on to tell me (granted, relatively briefly) about her red hair and the sometimes conflicted relationship she'd had with its color. I looked at her as she spoke—at her long auburn hair, shiny, glossy, and, despite her middle age, still cascading in long, well-behaved waves down her shoulders—and felt like throwing my big hardback copy of *Americanah* at her. Hard.

I STAND WHEN MY STYLIST directs me to. She faces me, up close, measuring with her fingers and her gaze the symmetry of the hair she has already cut. She pulls at the dry curls on either side of my head, calculating. I watch her as she looks at me. My face is close to her face; when I look away from it, above and below, I see her full cleavage emerging from her tight tank top, the black sketch of vines and birds tattooed on the brown skin of her naked arm and shoulder, the ultrafine strands of her shapely Afro. She is quiet and serious, all business, as she concentrates on cutting my curls evenly. My hair is a project that poses no problem for her. Not even a challenge.

RECENTLY THERE'S BEEN DISCUSSION about the difference between "inclusion" and "belonging." Belonging completes the idea of inclusion. Belonging means being a "part of." Not just included in a common space but actually contributing to that space, appreciated in that space, fitting in as a normal, natural part of that space—that place, room, club, organization, institution, town, country, culture, salon.

LATER, AFTER THE CUT IS DONE, my stylist guides me to the sink where she will finally wash and moisturize my hair. She uses a special conditioner that is gentle on curls, that protects waves and spirals rather than trying to subdue them. After she rinses the conditioner off, she asks me to bend forward from my seat and then shake my head—up and down, up and down, back and forth, back and forth. This, I gather, is to allow the different strands to curl together in the most natural way by using gravity. After carefully smoothing specialized gel onto the different sections of my head, she will put me under a huge, elongated dryer, where a mild heat will dry my hair with a minimum of blowing to prevent frizz.

No one has to tell her she must never brush my hair. No one has to tell her not to comb it after it dries. No one has to tell her not to use a harsh blow-dryer. She already knows. This is her specialty. She not only has expertise in the cutting and care of my hair, she herself has hair that is also curly-kinky-frizzy—i.e., *not straight*. In this way, we are the same.

ONE WAY I'VE HEARD BELONGING explained—specifically as opposed to inclusion—is through the idea of a party invitation. You've been invited to this party, and there's a place reserved for you at the table. It's set, like everyone else's, with a plate and cutlery and a glass for water or wine. Yet as you sit there, in your reserved seat, perhaps even with your name elegantly calligraphed on a card at the top of your place setting, no one talks to you. No one acknowledges you. You might as well be invisible. Not only are all the guests at the table talking to each other, they speak in another language, with words you can't understand no matter how hard you try, no matter how intensely you strain to make sense of them. They laugh at jokes you don't see coming and you can't recognize; they smile with a mutual sense of bonding and connection—yet regardless of effort or desire, of a desperate wanting, you cannot.

BUT HERE, IN THIS SALON, for the first time in my life, I feel like I belong.

Well, that's a bit of an exaggeration. It's the first time I've felt as if my *hair* belongs. And this feeling has come without fanfare; I did not expect it. I made the appointment at this specialized salon, with stylists who only cut curly hair and only cut it dry, merely on a whim and as an experiment—curious after all these years, a lifetime, really, of dealing with salons where curly hair, kinky hair, wild and unmanageable hair, was the outlier, the other, a shame, a disappointment, a burden.

Based on a True Story

THE CROW, BLACK-FEATHERED and intelligent-eyed, flies over the valley on its way to its destination. But something attracts its attention—maybe a shiny bauble or a dead mouse, or perhaps the gathering of humans, highly unusual in its timing and makeup. For it is summer vacation and this gathering is fairly large; in addition, there are more big humans than little ones on the town commons that primarily serves as a sports field for the small elementary school.

Whatever it is that draws its interest, the crow pauses mid-flight and selects an air current to glide on, weaving side to side in a leisurely manner as it takes in the scene below.

What does this crow see? It's a small town, a pretty town, a green leafy town with creeks and forests and ferns and moss. A fairy-book town, with hills and dales, meadows and trails, a town attractive in part because of the very school at its heart. There's a clearing down in the middle of the town, which itself is part of a large valley carved eons ago by the slow slide of loosened glaciers. Pines and redwoods and oaks surround the clearing, as well as streets and homes and a post office. The school shares this central area with the grassy commons, which today is covered with people, mostly families.

The crow sees the school's outdoor stage, reserved for plays and graduations, but does not understand that it holds an unusual set of actors—a priest, a sheriff, a mayor, a mother, a child. The people assembled on the grass face the stage, their expressions expectant. The priest (an Episcopalian one, as the crow would realize if it knew this town and its human culture well) seems to be the master of ceremonies. He introduces the others on the stage, he gives a speech, and the people in the audience listen and clap, smiles at the ready.

But at this point, alas, the crow begins to lose interest. It cannot know that this gathering is unprecedented in this quaint, affluent town, the inhabitants of which have modeled it after East Coast WASP-y wealth, with clapboard houses and discreet drives, as well as manicured lawns and wide porches wherever possible.

This is, after all, a rather unusual summer, a fact unbeknownst to the crow. It is the Summer of Hate, or, more accurately, the Summer of Hate Exposed: the Summer of 2020, the Summer of Race Riots, the Summer of the Murder of George Floyd.

Wait—the crow seems to have changed its mind. Perhaps wishing to rest before continuing on its journey, it flies down to land on a sturdy tree bough conveniently overlooking the action both on the grass and the stage.

If the crow were privy to the ins and outs of the human activity in this small town, it would know that this gathering is the brainchild of the priest, whose church, named after one of the Gospel writers, is located just across the street. On the front grounds of the church this same priest had placed several signs—some written in a childish hand, some in big bold print—proclaiming *Black Lives Matter, Say Their Names, All Are Welcome Here*.

The crow would also know, if suddenly infused with human understanding, that this assembly has been modeled, in its own strange, placid fashion, after rallies in Minneapolis and Los

Angeles and New York. It could be that the priest, in all his good intentions, wants to bring awareness to the townspeople, and to show the world that his parishioners care too. That they aren't all stereotypically conservative. That the people, not only of his church but also his town, are more than materialistic or entitled. That they are also capable of being thoughtful and compassionate.

The crowd gathered on the edge of the commons is mostly white, different shades of pale. Although ordinarily accustomed to overrunning the commons and the school grounds with privileged ease, the parents and the property owners and the taxpayers today exhibit a subtle air of discomfort. They don't know what to do. They felt compelled to assemble here, beckoned by the call of the local priest, by the flyer posted on the post office bulletin board, or maybe by an email from the town hall. These are the townspeople who pride themselves on being liberal; if they ever were Republicans, they were careful to say they were *fiscal* Republicans, implying that they too believed, at least in theory if not in practice, in equality for all. These more liberal townspeople—parents, teenagers, and older couples—mill around, voices somewhat subdued, shifting from foot to foot, glancing about, unsure as to the protocol for such an event. There are some small children playing on the swings and seesaw, of course. They don't know any better.

Why this sense, however vague, of unease? Why this aura, not usually felt in these parts? If we stay with the crow and give it, besides human understanding, that of gods and goddesses, then we can depend on its divine sight, like an infrared light, for a more accurate analysis of the scene. So now the crow is no longer a dumb animal, however curious of eye or agile of movement. It is as the gods on Olympus, viewing from above the antics of the humans far below. These gods see all, they know all.

So what does the crow now see? What does it now know?

Let's turn our attention back to the stage. On it there's a priest, a sheriff, a mayor, and a mother. There's a microphone and a baby. There's the crowd gathered before it. There is, in addition, a human observer and, as it happens, a storyteller. This storyteller feels inundated; nuggets of information, of sensation, of memory and prior knowledge, threaten to flood her mind. She's heard people with autism say that sometimes they experience an overwhelm—there are so many, too many, stimuli. In her case, she feels there aren't enough words to describe the scene in its entirety, in its intricacy and complexity. Vocabulary fails her.

Perhaps this is so—that the storyteller feels she faces a wordless void—because she is an actor in the same scene, not on the real-life school stage but in the audience, on the grassy commons, standing awkwardly, expectantly, somewhat anxiously, with the others. Squirrels collect acorns and nuts for the future, to take out in the dead, sterile winter and consume for energy and life. In this sense the woman too is like a squirrel—observing, looking, and watching in order to collect sights, sounds, and scenarios. What nuggets of knowledge, of sensation, does she find at this rally for mulling over later, for analysis and cataloging when there is time for reflection? For that is what it is. A rally. Definitely not a protest and not, of course—God forbid—a riot. There is no danger of that, for emotions run low here, at an ebb, scarcely a coaxed simmer. The stakes for this crowd are far too low.

To make things even more difficult for this storyteller, the nuggets of information and sensory stimuli that she collects for future consumption are not discrete; they are not singular, polished, rounded nuggets; they are instead jumbled and dirty, as if tumbled about for days by buffeting winds in rivers of mud. Trying to sort through nuggets that she could only perceive en masse, as if an avalanched pile of rocks and stones lying about willy-nilly, was to her like being in handcuffs, or quicksand, or even Harry Potter's Devil's Snare, where the more one struggles, the more one panics and thrashes about, the more the hold becomes stronger, tighter, and one chokes, with no possibility of moving, no room to breathe. She now likens the task of making sense of this scene to negotiating a giant spider's web—but not the pretty kind, hanging delicately from a bush at the edge of a trail, the kind that makes you stop on your hike and wonder at the delicate strands shining in the sun, drops of dew balanced precariously here and there like glass ornaments. Nor like the musty, dusty threads we call cobwebs, lightweight and decaying, all power and force sucked out by time and neglect, useless, cluttery, annoying at most. Instead she thinks of the webs in nightmares: The strong, entrapping kind. The enveloping, straitjacketing, mummifying kind. The kind that catch and snare, never to let go. She thinks of this kind as the sticky kind. The sticky, sticky web.

But she, the fifty-three-year-old woman, the storyteller, knows that the task of collecting and ordering to piece together a workable narrative has to be attempted. It is too irresponsible, too entitled, too hypocritical not to. If she can't sort it out right then and there, if she can't make complete sense of the scene of which she forms a part in the moment, then she can watch and listen and collect what her eyes and her ears take in, and maybe later, with time and effort, try to make a coherent whole of all the tangled, tumbled parts.

She thinks to herself that because this is the time of COVID scoffers and climate change deniers, of Trump vs. Greta, of droughts and wildfires, of mass incarceration of Black citizens, of police brutality and murder, of masks and anti-maskers, vaccines and anti-vaxxers, and of #MeToo and Black Lives Matter, these months and years could be called the time of the Great Binaries—Black vs. white, man vs. woman, patriarchy vs. humanism, Democrats vs. Republicans, homo vs. hetero, poor vs. rich, homeless vs. billionaire, drought vs. floods, Big Ag vs. the Suicide Belt . . . She senses that there is no room for shades of gray, for complexity and nuance, for thoughtfulness. Everywhere around her she sees only complication, entanglement, puzzles. The sticky web.

If we get down to brass tacks, since this is supposed to be a true story, then this is what she sees: The crowd. The people on the stage, one of whom is a mother holding a child. A man speaking into the microphone, thanking all for coming. He is the religious man. Then a man of the law speaking. Next a woman—she is the town mayor—speaking. Then, finally, the mother standing and approaching the mic.

She leans toward it, clutching her child. She thanks everyone in the audience, everyone listening, for the warmth and welcome she and her family and especially her adopted baby, the very one she holds in her arms, have received from them all since they moved to the town.

What is so strange, so interesting about this scene? Why does the storyteller sense, invisible yet all around her, that web?

There is someone else. Someone not from the town—a stranger, an outsider. Someone not white or brown, but Black. A large man, tall, wide-shouldered, and barrel-chested. He waits apart from the rest of the people gathered there; he seems to belong to no one. He stands out, with his height, his hue, his tight, colorful exercise spandex, his little leashed dog. He hovers on the periphery—in fact, the first time the woman spots him he is standing behind the trunk of a large pine tree, the very tree in which sits our crow.

Sad for him, ashamed for everyone else, the woman traces the man's movement as he paces from here to there at different times, taking in the speeches from the stage. Nobody speaks to him. He and his dog exist as if on their own island, a moat of fear or indifference or apathy surrounding them both. When she thinks of it several years later, the woman will consider the power of prejudice, how even the little fluffy dog, in this town of dog worshippers, could not entice anyone to approach the man, to ask the name of his pet, to kneel down and scratch between the puppy's ears.

She herself fails to approach the man, to engage him in conversation, because she fears seeming condescending or patronizing.

And the baby on the stage? The adopted baby? The one clutched to the maternal bosom as her mother looks out toward the pale faces of her audience and thanks them for their loving welcome of her family and child? This baby is also Black. Thus there are two clearly different people at the rally, this gathering to express outrage at the murder of a Black man by a white man, at a policeman's slow, knee-on-neck suffocation of an unarmed civilian: one the cute baby on the stage, brought there like an infant Messiah to be worshipped and adored, and one the adult male, pacing the margins, left alone, ignored. Forever after, whenever the woman thinks of the baby on the stage, she will think of the movie her young kids watched over and over where the king of the lions stands on the lip of a cliff, a natural rock stage, and holds out his newborn child to the other animals gathered below.

What does that make the man? The lone Black man?

How does one tell such a story? How does one position oneself within this narrative? Honestly and truthfully and directly? This effort, in and of itself, feels like a journey to the storyteller, a quest—but one so difficult, so labyrinthine, that it seems impossible.

This may be so (at least in part) because the storyteller belongs to her own class of humans—we'll call them the

Complicating Factors. She knows consciously, she feels viscerally, as she stands there in her leggings and lightweight jacket, in her flat shoes that accommodate the dirt and turf, with her family of other Complicating Factors—two sons and a husband—that she is indeed a Complicating Factor in this scene, which may feel like mere sound and fury, but that, to her, absolutely signifies something.

What is a Complicating Factor in this story? A CF is an in-betweener, a straddler of sides and cultures and races and religions, a citizen of La Frontera, someone familiar with the Borderlands. This woman and her family stand at this rally, on these commons, the soft grass yielding under their feet—not white, as are most of the people surrounding them, not Black, as are the girl baby and the solitary man. They are instead brown and beige, Peruvian and Syrian, Catholic and Muslim, immigrant and first-generation, mixed-race and not. Some of their ancestors modeled casual cultural racism, unquestioned biases, taken-for-granted privilege. Others were the objects of racism, conscious or unconscious, deliberate or facile. And for all of the woman's complicated factorship—part Latina, daughter of a Peruvian immigrant, a scholar and a part-time activist—she can pass as white. Assiduous application of sunscreen since her twenty-fifth year, when vanity made her wrinkle-phobic, has ensured that she presents to the world a pale face. But here she is—standing in what she feels is a battlefield of in-betweenness, a limbo of cultural transition—attending this parody of a rally.

She thinks of Edith Wharton, the author known for writing about her people with devastating judgment *and* loving compassion. If, as an expatriate, as an artist and a divorcée, Edith Wharton achieved the necessary distance to see, clear-eyed, both the horror and the beauty of her tribe, can the storyteller here at the rally claim that same right? Perhaps her borderland citizenship, her in-between status, gives her a special lens through which to critique a community gathered together to claim allyship with the poor and the beaten and the Black. Do the Borderlands count as sufficiently far from the center, as suitably outside the paradigm, for her to give a different perspective? Edith Wharton wrote with such a clear eye . . . the storyteller is envious. If only she had such clarity of vision. But she does not. She lacks the omniscience of the gods who might make sense of the paradoxes playing out this day both on the field and the stage.

When she saw the rally advertised—maybe at the post office, maybe on an email thread—this woman, with her complicated heritage and history, was ambivalent. At the same time that she felt encouraged, even inspired, by her small, conservative hometown putting this event together, she also felt skeptical. How aware could their collective consciousness be? The collective consciousness of this small, pretty town that was on average white, rich, and powerful?

Always part of the woman's own consciousness as observer, as witness, are the strands of the web, gummy and viscous: *A Peruvian grandmother, the visiting abuela, looks out the car window in the city across the bridge and, shaking her head, laments the clasped hands of a mixed-race couple . . . A son's redheaded classmate on the playground after school runs after an elderly couple walking by, the African parents of the only Black resident of the small town, yelling, "Are you hoboes?" . . . The same playground, a different classmate, blond and fair, calls another boy the n-word and his mother claims ignorance as to how to react . . . A Black Princeton student, visiting over the summer, is followed out of the local specialty food store by the white manager and falsely accused of stealing the magazine she holds in her hands . . . The very same Episcopalian priest who is the master of ceremonies at this gathering wants to offer shelter in his church to the homeless from the county, regardless of race, during the darkest hours of the coldest winter months but is outvoted by the townspeople . . . A brown friend, daughter of Indian immigrants, faces expulsion from a master's program for fully articulating the n-word when analyzing a hate crime . . . A Peruvian mother—daughter of the bigoted abuela, mother of the storyteller, and a fifty-year resident of this small town—is racially profiled by a local policeman for her darker skin and accented English . . .*

And today—in the town, surrounded by fellow residents who act, at least in this moment, as if they are liberal and progressive—the middle-aged woman, a Complicating Factor, has her doubts. The adoptive mother is white and wealthy and blends in with the other residents of this town. The adopted baby, the Black baby, has been put on exalted display. The solitary man, the Black man, at the same rally, in the same moment, big and tall and grown, continues to be alone and ignored. Ugly words flood her mind—*nominal, tokenism, performative, opportunism, exploitation, self-congratulation, hypocrisy . . .*

She wonders, being only human and not at all omniscient, what would happen if suddenly different signs and slogans appeared, as if by divine intervention, among this crowd that is almost one hundred percent white and largely within the economic one percent: *Capitalism Is Racist . . . Redistribute Wealth . . . There Is No Racial Justice Without Economic Justice . . . We Can't Breathe If We Can't Eat . . .*

But then she remembers the old truism: History is written by the victors. They hold the power to narrate what happened, to craft and mold what is happening. This rally, the actors on the stage, the words spoken into the mic, the gathering of families and couples and teenagers and children here on the town commons, is a play, a performance, a narrative. And one, it's clear to her, created and written by the victorious, by those who have won wars and battles and skirmishes, including the physical, social, psychological, and economic. There is no proof here of any loss, like injury or death, but instead the proof of victory is glazed over, gilded. The winners continue, still, to write history, in this case casting themselves as compassionate and democratic.

After the rally concludes, after the speeches and the applause, after the *awwws* toward the Black baby girl and the backs turned against the big Black stranger, some people leave, others stay. The storyteller and her family stay only long enough to see the families who crowd around the mother and her adopted child, praising the baby, cooing at her, using their cell phones to take selfies with Instagram-wide smiles by her side.

RECENTLY, I HEARD A QUOTE attributed to Napoleon: "What is history but a fable agreed upon?" This is what I feel I witnessed those three years ago, that summer of hate and violence and rioting. That the privileged white residents of my hometown were enacting a show; they were performing a history; they were creating a fable. There was no way, I sensed, to act, to speak, to intervene without getting more and more trapped in the stickiness of an invisible web. I was positioned in between, existing in a limbo. I believed myself politicized and aware, yet there I was, not an outside observer, not a temporary tourist or guest in this town, but a resident, the daughter of residents; regardless of where my family's (relatively limited) wealth came from, I still lived there, more often than not passing as white, always privileged in so many ways that others in this county and this country are not.

What I fear for myself: That I will fall into a trope, that I will become one of those people I'm familiar with through literature and history and my own observations. The Fatalist who gives up because everything is going to happen anyway, the good and the bad, the loving and the monstrous. The

Blinkered Woman who sees nothing but one goal—victory. Victory at all costs, personal, ethical, legal, or emotional. The Angry Person who claims, *Vengeance is mine,* only to become embittered, hateful, any "revenge" ricocheting back to herself. The Tireless Do-Gooder, who works and works and works, sacrificing self, health, and family, only to burn out, to disbelieve. Or the Cynic, the one who judges from the sidelines, sneering contempt, yet remains angered and outraged inside. There is no positive movement, no progressive change within these personas.

The signs and the slogans of that day at the small-town rally—*Black Lives Matter, Love Is Love, Kindness Is Everything*—they were empty. I must share in the shame that was and is the town's, that is both the bequest and the legacy of my identity as a citizen, not only of the town but also of the nation. Decades ago, Toni Morrison, single mother of two sons, writer and activist, Nobel Prize winner, said it straight: "Racism will disappear when it is no longer profitable." It seems to me that at least in these decades, in this cultural moment, maybe even in this era, there is no happy ending in sight. There is no neat way to end this story, to find a tidy moral with which to conclude. It's still ongoing, the mess and the struggle. The contestants on the larger national field are too many and too varied. Their beliefs—the dogmas that they cling to, the opinions that become concrete, fixed in a nanosecond—are part of that sticky, inescapable web.

Yet struggle and analyze and try I must. The sufferings and the injustices, both petty and great, must be recognized, addressed, felt, and rejected on some fundamental and continuing level. Otherwise—willed complacency or madness. Is this despair yet another strand of that sticky web?

I think back three decades, thirty-plus years, to my education. I think back and remember Gloria Anzaldúa: Philosopher

Queen of the Borderlands, Righteous Prophet of La Frontera. Her work, her life, her mandate: Explode the binaries. Step out of the box. Exit the paradigm. Create a Third Consciousness. The border identity, citizenship in La Frontera, what I call being a Complicating Factor—that space is full of contradictions and conflicts. It is that very friction that can enable, ultimately, with time and thought and commitment certainly, the creation of a new way of being.

Gloria Anzaldúa once wrote, "*Caminante, no hay puentes, se hace puentes al andar.*" For a long time I read the sentence incorrectly. Instead of "Traveler, there are no bridges, they are built as you walk," I read "*Cálmate,*" or "Calm down; although there are no bridges, they will be built as you walk." Either way, I felt that Gloria Anzaldúa spoke directly to me, a soothing sister, a calming voice. *Cálmate*—don't despair. Out of the very chaos, from the strands of the sticky web, something new can be fashioned.

Anda no más. Keep walking.

TO BE CONTINUED . . .

Source Acknowledgments

PARTS OF THIS BOOK were previously published, sometimes in slightly different form or with different titles, in the following publications: "Death Tax" in *ANMLY*, "The Raffle Prize Winner" in *Eclectica Magazine*, "Fear" in *Hippocampus Magazine*, "First Times" in *Raising Mothers*, "Death of a Patriarch" in *Sukoon Magazine*, "How to Hang an Ayah" in *Unlikely Stories Mark V*, and "The Dragon in the Garden" in *The Write Launch*.

This book includes quotes and references from Gloria Anzaldúa, *Borderlands/La Frontera: The New Mestiza*, Aunt Lute Books, 2006.

Acknowledgments

I'M SO GRATEFUL TO MY COMMUNITY of writers that includes teachers, educators, mentors, writing sisters, and accountability partners. My community has enriched my life and improved my writing, while serving as a source of support and encouragement and camaraderie. Thank you to my cozy feedback group at The Woven Tale Press. Thank you Vanessa Brown, Gina Baleria, Emily Cook, Chloé Cooper Jones, Nayomi Munaweera, and Anna Wong—my growing constellation of guiding stars. Thank you, again, to my ever-supportive sisters at She Writes Press. Thank you, always, to Natasha Singh, Brooke Warner, Allison K Williams, Linda Joy Myers, Allison Lane, Beth Kephart, Lisa Cooper Ellison, and Tamara Dean, my beloved coven of creatives. And thank you, last but never least, to Sonia Daccarett, my staunch supporter, always in my corner and at my side, *mi hermana en mestizaje*.

I need to thank more than individuals here; it is a necessity for a book like this one. I need to thank the cultures and communities that made me, and the research and writing and scholarship that helped explain me. I need to thank the Latino culture, the one that was before called "Hispanic"; I need to thank the cultures that are politicized—the Latina, the Chicana, those of *la frontera*, of the emigrant and the border crosser. I need to thank my mother's Peruvian culture; her hybrid parentage of Italian and Spanish and Peruvian; the culture taught to her in her Sagrado Corazon high school and at *la casa de las tías* every Sunday afternoon for the family luncheon; the culture she had to embody as an adult, that of immigrant, exile, a person known for having darker skin and accented English; and the culture of motherhood that embraced me and guided me and loved me unconditionally.

If I thank the communities and cultures of my mother, then I also need to thank my father's cultures, the ones he lived in until he was twelve in Berlin then Paris then Saint-Germain-des-Prés. His mother's: forever staunchly British, proper and schoolmarmish, strict and unyielding. His father's: the journalist's, the writer's, the diary keeper's, the army officer's, the reader's. My father's straightforward, undeviating alliance to his own ethical code. Then, of course, UC Berkeley's culture, where I first found the language for my thoughts and feelings, and the University of Washington's, where I learned the practice of my evolving philosophies. And the cultures of all the places I've lived in and married into and visited and navigated—Ecuador's and Peru's and the Philippines' and Brazil's and Syria's, and that of the United States. Those, as well, of England, Canada, Egypt, Turkey, Spain, and Italy. Also, always and absolutely, the intersecting cultures of feminism and mestizaje. Because each of these is a culture that has shaped me in its unique way, I acknowledge them all as instrumental to the writing of this book.

About the Author

MARIANNA MARLOWE is a Latina writer of creative nonfiction that explores issues of gender identity, feminism, cultural hybridity, intersectionality, and more. Her short memoir has been published in *Narrative Magazine, Hippocampus Magazine, The Woven Tale Press, Eclectica Magazine, Sukoon Magazine,* and *The Acentos Review* among others. She lives in the San Francisco Bay Area.

Author photo © Stephanie Mohan Creative Portraiture

Looking for your next great read?

We can help!

Visit www.shewritespress.com/next-read
or scan the QR code below for a list
of our recommended titles.

She Writes Press is an award-winning
independent publishing company founded to
serve women writers everywhere.

SWP